ESSENTIALS OF EVANGELISM

The Bob Jones University Lectures on Evangelism for 1958

by

Tom Malone, D.D.

Foreword by Dr. Bob Jones, Jr.

http://www.baptistbiblebelivers.com/

www.solidchristianbooks.com

Contents

FOREWORD 3
CHAPTER ONE PREACHING TO WIN THE LOST 4
CHAPTER TWO WHY THIS GENERATION SHOULD EVANGELIZE THE WORLD 17
CHAPTER THREE THE HOLY SPIRIT 32
CHAPTER FOUR WHAT HAPPENED ON THE DAY OF PENTECOST? 43
CHAPTER FIVE WHY MANY CHURCHES OF AMERICA ARE DEAD AND FORSAKEN 56
CHAPTER SIX HAVE FAITH IN GOD 70
CHAPTER SEVEN WHY FEW ARE SAVED, MULTITUDES ARE LOST 83
CHAPTER EIGHT EVANGELISM AND SOUL-WINNING A DAILY BUSINESS 96
CHAPTER NINE WHAT IS CLOSEST TO THE HEART OF JESUS? 105
CHAPTER TEN HOW A CHURCH SHOULD PREPARE FOR A REVIVAL CAMPAIGN 118
CHAPTER ELEVEN HOW A CHURCH SHOULD CHOSE AND TREAT AN EVANGELIST 127
CHAPTER TWELVE HOW AN EVANGELIST SHOULD TREAT A CHURCH AND PASTOR 132

FOREWORD

This is the eighth volume of the Lectures on Evangelism delivered annually at Bob Jones University.

As President of Bob Jones University, I feel a tremendous responsibility each year to select carefully the man who shall be invited to deliver the Lectures. I try to select either a man whom God has singularly blessed in the conducting of Scriptural evangelistic campaigns, a man who is known as an authority on evangelism and is engaged in the promotion of such work, or a pastor who is noted for a strong, evangelistic and soul-winning ministry in his own church and in the conducting of special evangelistic meetings for other pastors.

Dr. Malone has built in the last few years one of the largest and strongest churches on this Continent. It has been built around his own evangelistic ministry and personal soul-winning efforts. He is the founder and head of a Christian day school and Seminary. He is the editor of a paper which is both uncompromising in its orthodoxy and evangelistic in its emphasis.

I am convinced that any man who loves the Lord and is interested in the salvation of souls and the reviving of the Church will approve my choice of Dr. Malone as the Lecturer for 1958. I am convinced, too, that the excellent quality of the setup and printing of this volume is an indication of an equally good choice in the publisher.

In February, 1959, James A. Stewart, Scotch evangelist, internationally known for his powerful preaching, his Scriptural approach, and his uncompromising stand for the fundamentals of the Faith, will deliver to the students and faculty of Bob Jones University the next annual series of Lectures on Evangelism. These will be published in due course so that others outside the University family may share in the same sort of instruction and blessing which we are sure they will find in the present volume.

Bob Jones, Jr.

President Bob Jones University

CHAPTER ONE PREACHING TO WIN THE LOST

II Timothy 3:1-7, 4:1-5

My text for this message is made up of two short but challenging phrases,

"**Preach the word**" (II Timothy 4:2).

"**Do the work of an evangelist**" (II Timothy 4:5).

I have it in my heart to speak especially to the preachers. I don't want you to feel, however, if you are not a preacher that I am not talking to you. I might say that I have it on my heart to speak especially to all who are interested in propagating the gospel to the ends of the earth, carrying out the great commission of our Lord Jesus and winning the lost of the earth for whom He died.

You know these are challenging days. I need not remind you of that. One of the amazing things to me about the Bible is how minutely and accurately it describes these last days in which you and I live. Here is a passage of Scripture that we have read that challenges the heart of any true Christian. It tells us something about the characteristics of the last evil days before the coming of our Lord Jesus to receive His church unto Himself. There are many enemies to the gospel today and to preachers and Christian workers and to fundamental Bible-believing soul-winning churches.

The Bible plainly teaches that in this day in which you and I live men will have "**a form of godliness but deny the power thereof**." There never has been a generation of preachers, there never has been a generation of Christians that has seen so vividly the fulfillment of that part of God's Word—"**a form godliness but denying the power thereof.**" There is worldliness and modernism on every hand, wickedness in high places, wickedness everywhere scattered across the face of the earth. These are challenging days. They are challenging days for missionaries; they are challenging days for preachers; they are challenging days for ever single Christian.

I find that in many instances God's people sometimes get discouraged in trying to get the job done before the coming of the Lord. We find even in Bible times that Christian leaders and men of God reached days of great discouragement. Take, for instance, that mighty prophet Elijah. Never has a man risen to greater heights, never has a man enjoyed greater power of God than Elijah did yonder on Mt. Carmel.

Elijah challenged four hundred false prophets of Baal, preachers of modernism. He prayed; God opened the heavens and fire fell. He slew the prophets. He set them at nought. He vindicated the cause of God. He proved that they were evil, that modernism was, wrong and of the Devil. Oh, to what heights he arose. Never was there a character in the Bible outside the Lord Jesus Christ who ever rose to such a pinnacle of power with God as Elijah did on Mt. Carmel. But only a few hours later there came a message from wicked Jezebel, the godless queen, that **"before the sun goes down tomorrow night, I'm going to cut off your head as you cut off the heads of my prophets of Baal**."

We see Elijah discouraged and defeated and running yonder a day's journey into the woodland, sitting down under a tree and praying to God that he might die. Yes, the Devil knows how to put Satanic pressure upon the people of God and how to discourage if he can the Christian worker, missionary, preacher, evangelist, and pastor. We need today, I think, as never before the power of God. We need today as never before to know simply and plainly if we can by God's help and grace, how from the Bible we can get the equipment and power from God to get the job done.

I never will forget hearing about a friend of mine who is preacher and has done a wonderful work but who one day reached a place of great discouragement as a preacher (If I should call his name some of you would know him). He said to his little church that didn't seem to be growing, "I'm going to resign. It is not fair to you to have a pastor who cannot deliver the goods and win the lost. I'm defeated and discouraged."

He went away to a conference on evangelism such as this. He came in a little late and the seats were all filled. A great crowd had gathered. He leaned back against the wall and dropped his chin upon his chest. In a moment a preacher got up and began to preach, and God began to speak to him.

- He saw that night in the message that God is greater than all opposition.
- He saw that night that God is greater than all his inabilities.
- He saw that night how it would be possible for the power of God to come on his life so that his life would be a mighty instrument in the hands of God.

He stood there and wept as the Spirit of God searched deep down in his soul, and that night standing against the wall, he said, "Dear Lord, if You will give me another chance, if You will help me, if You will stir my soul tonight, if You will come upon me and clothe me with the power of God, I will be a soul winner."

He sent a wire back to his little church, and the wire read something like this: "You are going to have a new preacher next Sunday. Be sure to be there to hear him."

The next Sunday morning from all outward appearances the same preacher walked into the pulpit, but he wasn't the same. He walked into that pulpit with a burning heart; he walked into that pulpit with a broken heart; he walked into that pulpit weeping over sinners, and he has been winning them to God ever since.

I will tell you, my friends, I believe with all my soul that there are not enough demons in hell and that Satan does not have enough power to overcome the Christian who is fully consecrated and yielded and sold out to God. The question so often comes to me and I know it does to other preachers, "How can we preach in this age? How can we got the job done that God wants us to do?" I want to give you four ways that I believe that preachers ought to preach and Christians ought to witness.

I. WE NEED TO PREACH AND WITNESS WITH REALITY

I believe with all my soul that we ought to witness and preach with a reality in our message. We ought to believe what we are preaching, it ought to grip our hearts to such an extent that every time we sing, or preach, or witness whether people believe the message or not, whether they agree with what we say or not, they will be bound to admit, "There is a preacher or there is a missionary or there is a young man or a young woman who really believes what he or she is singing or what he is preaching." We ought to preach with reality.

The other day a lady said to me, "Brother Tom, I want you to go and talk to a man in the hospital who has not been saved and who needs the Lord. This man has been a very successful man; he has a very important job in one of the automobile factories here in the city, but he is lost."

I went to the hospital, asked for the number of the room, and went to the room, but there was an empty bed. I said to one of the people, in the room, "Where is Mr. So-and-So?"

"They said, "He is down in X-ray. He will be back in a few minutes."

I waited awhile but he didn't come. The next day I went back and said, "Where is Mr. So-and-So?"

"He's down in X-ray."

I waited a few minutes and he didn't come back. This may seem like a fairy story to you, but I went back the third time and said, "Where is Mr. So-and-So?"

They again replied, "He is down in X-ray."

I began to wonder if all they had been doing to the poor guy was X-raying him for three days. Then I asked, "Where is X-ray?" They told me where it was, and the thought came to me, "If the Devil wants so badly for you not to see him and not to witness to him and not to talk to him, surely he needs Christ, surely he can be won, surely God wants me to reach him, and I will."

I went down to the X-ray room. They brought him out in a moment and I talked to him in the hallway. Along came someone rolling him down the hall, and I followed them awhile. I went back up into his room and talked with him. This is what I want to tell you. I said to him "Friend, are you a Christian? Are you a saved man?"

He said, "I'm a member of the church, Mr. Malone." He told me what church and how long he had been a member of it.

I asked, "But are you saved? Do you know Christ? Do you know where you are going when you die? If today were to be your last day do you know where you are going to spend eternity?"

He looked at me and said, "Mr. Malone, I have heard you preach on the radio, and I know that you believe something I do not believe. From what I have heard you say, I think you believe that out yonder in eternity there is a place called heaven."

I replied, "Yes, I do."

He said. "I have heard you preach about heaven."

I said, "Yes, I have preached about heaven and I believe that it is real."

He said, "I do not believe that people have a real body in heaven or hell and that they are going to be able to be seen and to walk and to talk in a literal body. I don't believe it is going to be real as you say it is. Do you really believe it?"

I said, "Yes, I believe it with all my heart. With all my soul I believe as Jesus taught that every lost man and woman, boy or girl who has not been born by God's Holy Ghost is forever lost and will spend eternity in hell."

This man reached out and put his hand on my arm and looked deep into my face and said, "Mr. Malone, if that is true, it is mighty serious business."

I prayed, "Oh, God, give to my heart and the heart of every Christian the seriousness of the unbelieving man."

My friends, I will tell you today, it is true, and it is serious business. Multitudes are lost. They are lost in your city; they are lost all over America; they are lost on every mission field, and we need to enter into the Holy Presence of God in travail of soul and in earnest supplication and prayer until we can go out with a message and the people can say, "Those people believe what they are preaching." We need to preach with tremendous reality.

It is said that some years ago in England there was a great actor giving a reading in a room filled with people. Someone suggested to him that he give the 23rd Psalm. He asked, "Do you really want me to?"

An old clergyman stood up and said, "Yes, Sir. Give the 23rd Psalm."

It is said that the great actor with the most precise intonations and the finest of elocution began to recite. When he had finished, the people smiled and nodded their heads and applauded. Then the actor said, "I want that elderly preacher to give it."

That gray haired preacher rose like a giant for God and began, "**The Lord is my shepherd**." He walked with God in the green meadows; he walked with God beside the still waters; he walked with God down in the dark valley that came out on the bright side, and finally with his face turned toward heaven he closed, "**Surely goodness and mercy shall follow me all the days of my life: and I will dwell in the house of the Lord for ever**."

He sat down. Nobody applauded but heads were bowed and people were weeping.

The great actor arose and said, "The difference between me and this preacher is that I knew the Psalm but he knew the Shepherd."

My friend, our preaching and witnessing must be done with a reality that will grip the hearts of people. It must not be vague. It must not be filled with doubt. We must preach and witness so that the lost of earth shall take knowledge of us that **"we have been with Jesus."**

Listen, the world today has enough doubt without getting any more from you and from me. We must preach with the tone of reality.

II. WE MUST PREACH AND WITNESS WITH COURAGE

This is no day for the faint hearted. This is the day for the 300 who will go all the way with Gideon. This is no day for the cowardly. This is the day for John the Baptist who preached the truth and let the chips fall where they would. This is the day when men must be willing to lose their heads if need be for the sake of the gospel.

I read some years ago of a wonderful thing that happened in Jacksonboro, Georgia, and was published in the *St. Louis Star-Times* with the dateline October 31, 1949. The article went like this, "The lone survivor of Jacksonboro – the accursed town that was – is dead.

Out of that once damned, now desolate region on Beaver Creek came word today that Richard Bryant, 105-year-old, had died Friday night.

He was the only man alive who saw the terrible curse of a little, hunchbacked, itinerant minister, Lorenzo Dow, come true. He saw the once bustling town disappear, house by house, store by store, until but one house remained – the house specifically spared by Dow. When Bryant was 3 years old, he saw the residents give up in despair at the freaks of fire, water and wind and move five miles away to found another town, Sylvania.

It was in 1794 that Jacksonboro, half way between Augusta and Savannah, had been founded. For 36 years the town went its boisterous way. Then in 1830 Dow drifted down and called upon its citizens to repent. People laughed. They pelted him with eggs, and they would not let him preach. The tormented little minister with the burning eyes turned this way and that until a powerful man, Seaborn Goodall, gave him sanctuary in his house. When Dow strode to meet his tormentors again the following day, a mob drove him to a rustic bridge and bade him never return.

Scornfully, Dow paused on the span, turned and swore that God would bring swift vengeance, the same that overtook Sodom and Gomorrah. The townsfolk laughed again.

But then, unaccountably, fires broke out, windstorms tore off roofs, the placid creek through the middle of the town became wild and unruly, sweeping away homes in flash floods. The remaining settlers finally gave up and moved. Time removed all traces of the town but the Goodall place. Here Bryant was born."

Friends, have the courage to stand like a Daniel, to suffer like a Joseph and God will stand by you. God help us to have such convictions today as Christians that we can say to God and to men until the mountains crumble to dust, "I will never lower the blood-stained flag of the cross."

III. WE NEED TO PREACH AND WITNESS WITH COMPASSION

We must preach with compassion. You know, my friends, there is absolutely no substitute for compassion in the work of God. You may have everything else in the world. You may have the greatest talent a person could be endowed with; you may have the greatest mind possible, but there is no substitute for a compassionate heart in the work of God.

Let me tell you, preachers, if you can preach and preach and preach and preach and never shed a tear, never have your heart broken, never know what it means to travail and agonize with an agony akin to that which Jesus had in Gethsemane, if you can preach without tears and compassion, you are going to do a lot of preaching without souls.

Oh, I see Jesus coming yonder on the Mt. of Olives and looking down on the city of Jerusalem and from a broken heart crying, "**O Jerusalem, Jerusalem, how often would I have gathered thee to Myself as a hen gathers her chickens, but ye would not**." The Bible says He beheld the city and wept over it. I can tell you, my friends, if we are going to move people toward God; we are going to have to have some tears.

Jesus had compassion. We read in the Word of God, "**But when he saw the multitudes, he was moved with compassion on them, because they fainted, and were scattered abroad, as sheep having no shepherd.**" Then saith He unto his disciples, "**The harvest truly is plenteous, but the labourers are few; Pray ye therefore the Lord of the harvest, that he will send forth labourers into his harvest.**"

The lost multitudes did something to Jesus. They moved Him to tears. They stirred His heart. He was moved by their great numbers, their weakness and sin. He was moved because they fainted and were scattered and had no shepherd to love them and win them. He sees the lost multitudes of earth as a great harvest field and challenges the children of God to pray, to give, to go. Paul had tears. He "**ceased not to warn every one night and day with tears**" (Acts 19:31).

I hear people talk today about why so many folks are going into false cults and other false and erroneous "isms". I think I know the answer.

I am a fundamentalist. I believe like every fundamental, Bible-believing Christian believes, but I want to tell you that people want some warmth. They want a heart-felt Christianity; they want some tears; they are tired of technicalities; they are tired of hair-splitting. People want a message with some warmth and fervor and love in it.

I wish God would give us what Mr. Whitefield had. It is said that he preached two hours on the morning of his death. He climbed the stairs one night with a little candle in his hand and started into his bedroom. It is said that out of the window he saw the multitudes and heard them cry, "Come out, Mr. Whitefield, and preach to us some more."

It is said that the old preacher walked out on the little balcony, held the candle for two hours, poured out his soul and preached with tears the gospel to the multitudes. With the candle burning low, he closed the door and walked off the balcony back into his bedroom. That night the candle of his life burned out to shine no more on this earth. Oh, God help us to burn out for Jesus with a broken heart. God give us tears and help us to see men and women lost around the world. God help us to see today the agony, the sin, the remorse, the affliction, the trouble that can be remedied by a warm and stirring message of the dynamic gospel of the Son of God. We need to preach with some tears. God give us a broken heart. God give us tears.

I heard one preacher say that he used to be ashamed to weep and so he prayed, "Oh, God, help me not to embarrass myself and others by weeping over sinners; help me to preach without tears." He said for a long time he did. Then one day he said he went back on his knees to God and prayed, "Give me back my tears." He said that God did and that he never wanted to be without them again.

If we can see the horrors of hell, the miseries of sin, the awful depths of God's infinite wrath and judgment and not have a broken heart, then we are evidently following Jesus from afar off. God gives us tears. Let me tell you, my friend, if God can give us the vision that we ought to have, if God will help us to see things as they are and we cannot Weep, God have mercy on us!

J. Wilbur Chapman told of visiting Sam Hadley in his great work in the slums in the city of New York He said one day, "Sam, I want you to show me tonight the slums of this city and these human derelicts without God. I want to see these sinners in the rough. It is said that that night J. Wilbur Chapman and Sam Hadley walked together down in the slums. Mr. Chapman wrote about it and said he had never seen such awful conditions. He saw men lying prostrate on the side walks and in the gutters. He heard the curses of the lost men and women; he heard the shrieks and groans and all that goes with drunkenness and debauchery and lust and sin. He heard it all. As they walked along Mr. Chapman said they came under a street light and all of a sudden he heard Sam Hadley cry, "Oh, oh, oh!"

He turned around and asked, "Sam, have you had a seizure? Have you had an attack?" He said in that street light he saw Sam Hadley's face lifted toward heaven and heard him cry, "Oh, God, give me these souls."

J. Wilbur Chapman said, "My heart broke."

My friends, may God give us a taste of what John Knox had when he cried, "Oh, God, give me Scotland or I die."

God's Holy Book says, **"He that goeth forth and weepeth, bearing precious seed, shall doubtless come again with rejoicing, bringing his sheaves with him**."

Let me tell you:

- You take your intellect; give me the tears;
- You take your theology, give me the tears;
- You take our hair-splitting, give me the tears;
- You take your technicalities, give me the tears.

Oh, God, give us church members that can weep over souls lost and without God.

IV. WE MUST PREACH AND WITNESS IN THE POWER OF THE HOLY SPIRIT

Then in the fourth and last place, we should preach and witness in the power of the Holy Spirit. Jesus said, **"Ye shall receive power, after that the Holy Ghost is come upon you: and ye shall be witnesses unto me both in Jerusalem, and in all Judea, and in Samaria, and unto the uttermost part of the earth"** (Acts 1:8). Now watch, **"Ye shall be witnesses unto me after the Holy Ghost is come upon you."** You know, my friends, the thing we preachers need is to be fired up. We preachers need the power of the Holy Ghost.

In the 20th Chapter of the book of John you read of the meeting of Jesus with the disciples after the resurrection, and you read how that He breathed on them and said, **"Receive ye the Holy Ghost."**

I sometimes feel that much of my ministry is without the breath of God. Oh, for the breath of God! Oh, for the power that comes from above!

In Exodus Chapter 32 we read of Israel's idolatrous sin in connection with the golden calf. This awful sin broke the heart of Moses and grieved the heart of God. God plagued the people and said, **"I will**

send an angel before thee" (Exodus 32:34) to lead them into the land of promise, but God said, "**I will not go up in the midst of thee**" (Exodus 33:3).

Moses continued to plead with God and stand in the gap. He prayed, "**Yet now, if thou wilt forgive their sin—; and if not, blot me, I pray thee, out of thy book which thou hast written**" (Exodus 32:32). What a tremendous prayer of intercession that was. Then God said to Moses, "**My presence shall go with thee and I shall give thee rest**" (Exodus 33:14), and Moses responded with this statement, "**If thy presence go not with me, carry us not up hence**" (Exodus 33:15). Oh! That is what we need, the wonderful presence of God. We should stay in the holy place of prayer until we are saturated and empowered with His Holy Presence.

My friends, we need the breath and presence of God. Tom Malone needs, every preacher needs, every missionary needs, every Christian, if he is going to witness effectively for God to win the lost, needs to go into the presence of God and stay until his face is shining when he comes out.

Moses waited in the presence of God in the quietness of that inner chamber until there was a holy glow on his countenance.

It was said of the great Paderewski, that great interpreter of music that he had this unusual characteristic. It is said that on the afternoon of his great concerts, he would go to the huge hall where he was to perform several hours before the performance was to start, He would go into all parts of the building. He would look in all the rooms and alcoves. He would check over all the equipment. Then he would go back yonder into a room and close the door having given orders that he was to see no one. No one was to open that door until the hour of the performance. The manager would come and without a word in absolute silence would take him by the hand and lead him out before the crowd to sit at the piano. It is said that if that manager spoke one word that the great Paderewski would turn on him and go back into the room and stay for another few minutes of silence. He wanted to meditate until that music gripped his soul, until it fairly saturated his mind.

My friends, we need to stay in the secret chamber until the power of God vibrates in every fiber of our being. We ought not to be afraid to talk about the Holy Spirit; we ought not to be afraid to pray for His power.

After John Knox had preached in the power of God, someone came down the aisle and met him and said, "Mr. Knox, you preached today as if you came right out of the throne room."

Mr. Knox bowed his head in humility and said, "Perhaps I did."

God help us to live as if we have come right out of the throne room of the very presence of God. If we are to change the discords of sin into heavenly melodies of love, if we are to touch the souls of men, our own souls must be in tune with the Infinite. God help us to preach and witness with reality, with courage, with compassion, and with the power and demonstration of the Holy Spirit.

CHAPTER TWO WHY THIS GENERATION SHOULD EVANGELIZE THE WORLD

TEXT: "**NOW then we are ambassadors for Christ, as though God did beseech you by us: we pray you in Christ's stead, be ye reconciled to God**" (II Corinthians 5:20).

In this great fifth chapter of Second Corinthians, we have five tremendous reasons why every believer should serve God with all his heart and soul.

1. *The Judgment Seat of Christ*

"**For we must all appear before the judgment seat of Christ; that every one may receive the things done in his body, according to that he hath done, whether it be good or bad**" (II Corinthians 5:10).

2. *The Terror of the Lord*

"**Knowing therefore the terror of the Lord, we persuade men; but we are made manifest unto God; and I trust also are made manifest in your consciences**" (II Corinthians 5:11).

3. *The Love of Christ*

"**For the love of Christ constraineth us; because we thus judge, that if one died for all, then were all dead**" (II Corinthians 5:14).

4. *The Changed Life*

"**Therefore if any man be in Christ, he is a new creature: old things are passed away; behold, all things are become new**" (II Corinthians 5:17).

5. *The Appointment as Ambassadors*

"**Now then we are ambassadors for Christ, as though God did**

beseech you by us: we pray you in Christ's stead, be ye reconciled to God" (II Corinthians 5:20).

If any Christian will carefully meditate upon these five soul-stirring truths, he will see what a heavy responsibility we have. We are God's ambassadors and representatives to make Jesus and His saving grace known to the ends of the earth. We have more equipment with which to get the job accomplished than any previous generation has ever had. We have the use of the radio, the television, the airplane, the printed page and many other advantages that even our previous generation did not enjoy.

With all these advantages, however, we still will not evangelize our generation, we will not win multitudes to Christ, and we will not please our Lord Jesus unless individual believers are stirred and moved to concentrated, consecrated, cooperative action. The evangelization of the world depends upon the church of today. God uses people! God needs real men and women today who have courage, faith and character. He needs men and women who are sold out to the gospel and who are willing to hazard their lives for the sake of that message, by God's infinite grace and power we succeed in evangelizing our generation, it will be done through personal evangelism or person to person contact.

"Now then we are ambassadors for Christ as though God did beseech you by us."

Quite a good many years ago—I don't know exactly how many—something happened down in the state of Alabama. When I heard of it many years later, it was a blessing to my heart; but it didn't mean much to me then as it has come to mean in later years. It had to do with a Christian sowing the seed and seeking to win a lost soul to Jesus Christ.

I heard my grandfather tell of one of the greatest things that ever happened in his life. He died at the age of 92 years and went triumphantly to heaven. He and my grandmother were in their 70th wedding year. He had seen a lot of things happen; and he had seen a lot of the world. Not many people have seen 90 to 100 years of life such as he had.

When I was first converted, I heard my grandfather tell something that was a blessing to me to hear, and I'll never forget it as long as I live. He was an unsaved man until he was past 70; or at least he was living in sin and not right with God. He told me how, years ago when he was a younger man and strong and healthy, he took a crew of men and was building a section of the great Jackson highway that runs north and south right through the state of Alabama. He was away from home except on the weekends. They built little shacks by the side of the road and the men dwelt in just these little shacks while they were building the highway. My grandfather had one of his own where he slept at night and ate his meals—just a little shack like a tool shed.

One night after a hard day's work he was in that little shack. He was tired and was preparing something to eat. Immediately after he ate every night, he went to bed. Just as he was preparing supper, a fine-looking man whom he knew from the little town of Russellville, Alabama, walked in. He was a wonderful Christian man by the name of Scharnockle.

Mr. Scharnockle said to my grandfather, "Will, I came to talk to you about something I have on my heart."

My grandfather didn't have any idea what this man had on his heart. Grandfather had been a sheriff and was well-known as an unsaved and wicked man, a man who was strong of body and felt no need of God.

Mr. Scharnockle said, "Will, I have come tonight to talk to you about Jesus Christ. I'm a Christian and I've been praying that you might be saved. A lot of people are afraid to talk to you, but I knew that with God's help I could come into this little shack tonight, sit down as a child of God and tell you what the Lord has done for me and how God saved my soul. I'm interested in you, and I know that you are not too wicked for God to save."

Grandfather didn't like it very much, but he said, "Scharnockle, this is not very good food. I don't know how to cook very well, but you sit down and eat with me."

This refined and wonderful Christian man sat at the table in the little shack and ate of the beans and very common food that my grandfather had fixed. They sat at the table and finally my grandfather said, "Well, you know I have to get up early. I have a hard day tomorrow, and I'm going to have to turn in, Scharnockle."

Mr. Scharnockle said, "If you don't mind, Will, I think I'll spend the night with you. I told my family I might not be home, and I think I'll spend the night here if you don't mind."

Grandfather answered, "Well, we sleep on pallets" (most of you don't know what a pallet is. It's just a blanket or something thrown on the floor). "If you can put up with it, then all right."

My grandfather threw a quilt over in one corner and a quilt over in another. He lay on one and Mr. Scharnockle on the other. The old kerosene lamp was blown out and they lay there in the dark.

Mr. Scharnockle told my grandfather about the love of Jesus for a sinner such as he. Grandfather lay in the dark hearing the gospel.

Years went by. Mr. Scharnockle died and went to heaven. Years ago when I was preaching as a young preacher in a little school building in north Alabama, my grandfather with my grand-mother on his arm came down the aisle and publicly confessed Christ as their personal Saviour.

They united with the church, and until God took away much of his eyesight a short time ago, he read the Bible two or three hours a day and talked to everybody that came about the love of God. He read the New Testament through 28 times and The Old Book, as he called it, through several times before he died.

I start my message with that story because I have on my heart but one theme — the Christian as a witness and as a soul winner for Jesus Christ. If there is anything made plain in the New Testament, or in all the Bible for that matter, it is that God's most wonderful method of making Christ known to the ends of the earth is the method of one individual telling another.

It is a strange thing to me that it is so hard to get God's people to do this. The communists do it. That is the way communism has engulfed a large portion of the world One communist has made a communist out of another man. That ii the way political parties grow. There is no trouble about that. One democrat makes a democrat out of another man; one republican makes a republican out of another man. The Bible has made it clear that one Christian has God's grace and power in his life to make a Christian out of another man.

I would like to give you a few exciting reasons now why we should lend every energy and exert every possible effort to evangelize the entire world in our generation.

I. WE ARE COMMANDED TO DO SO IN THE WORD OF GOD

We find this command in many places in the Bible. "**But ye shall receive power, after that the**

Holy Ghost is come upon you: and ye shall be witnesses unto me both in Jerusalem, and in all Judea, and in Samaria, and unto the uttermost part of the earth" (Acts 1:8).

The parting command of Jesus to the disciples was, "**Go ye into all the world, and preach the gospel to every creature**" (Mark 16:15). Notice the closing verse of the gospel of Mark, "**And they went forth, and preached everywhere, the Lord working with them, and confirming the word with signs following**" (Mark 16:20).

Yes, the early Christians "**went forth and preached everywhere**"! This command has never been withdrawn or changed, the church should still be going forth and preaching everywhere even until this good hour.

I heard a friend of mine tell sometime ago of a fine, strong, healthy country boy who got saved in his church. The parents of this boy were quite well to do. They owned hundreds of acres of land and the best of farm equipment. They had willed it all to this boy, their only son.

One day the boy said to his parents, "I have lost all interest in the farm and all this land and cattle and equipment. Since I have been saved, my thoughts are only for the souls of men. I must leave you and go away to a Christian school and study for the ministry."

The parents were heartbroken. They said, "Son, we had hoped to leave our fortune with you, and we had hoped that your name would always be on these buildings and that you would carry on our family traditions."

The parents went to see this preacher friend of mine and said, "You have ruined our boy. You have made a fanatic out of him. In fact, we think he has been affected mentally."

The preacher said to the parents, "Your boy is not ruined and he is not crazy. He has had a glimpse of Jesus who died for all his sins, and he has seen the lost multitudes of earth who have no Saviour, no Shepherd, and no hope. He has had a glimpse of eternity. He has had a heavenly vision; and he wants to be able to say when he comes down to the sunset of life, '**I was not disobedient to that heavenly vision.**'"

To show no interest in soul winning, to have no active part in world evangelism is to be guilty of the awful sin of disobedience. God's Word says, " **To him that knoweth to do good and doeth it not, to him it is sin**." If you know you ought to win souls and you are not winning them, then you are sinning against God and you are guilty of a flagrant violation of God's Holy Word!

"**Now then we are ambassadors for Christ, as though God did beseech you by us: we pray you in Christ's stead, be ye reconciled to God**" (II Corinthians 5:20).

II. THE SECOND COMING OF CHRIST EXCITES US TO WIN THE LOST

Out of the 7,959 verses in the 27 books of the New Testament, no less than 330 of them have direct reference to the fact that Jesus is coming back again.

1. *Jesus Himself said He would return.*

"**Let not your heart be troubled: ye believe in God, believe also in me. In my Father's house are many mansions: if it were not so, I would have told you. I go to prepare a place for you. And if I go and prepare a place for you, I will come again, and receive you unto myself; that where I am, there ye may be also**" (John 14:1-3).

He also said in the 24th chapter of Matthew that He would come again. In this chapter, we have the inspired record of His longest prophetical discourse. In answer to the anxious inquiry of his disciples; as to "**what shall be the sign of thy coming and of the end of the world**," He speaks with divine solemnity concerning the close of this age of their church. He rings down the curtain on this dispensation of grace. Meditate today, Christian friends, upon His words in Matthew 24:44, "**Therefore be ye also ready for in such an hour as ye think not the Son of man cometh**."

2. *The angels of heaven said the Lord Jesus would come back.*

The first chapter of the book of Acts tells of His ascension and gives this! account of the heavenly messenger who came down as He went up "**And while they looked stedfastly toward heaven as he went up, behold two men stood by them in white apparel; Which also said, Ye men of Galilee, why stand ye gazing up into heaven? This same Jesus, which is taken up from you into heaven, shall so come in like manner as ye have seen him go into heaven**" (Acts 1:10-11).

3. *Paul said Jesus would return.*

The doctrine of the Second Coming of Christ literally saturates and permeates all of his letters.

To the Roman believers he wrote, "**And that, knowing the time that** now it is high time to awake out of sleep: for now is our salvation nearer than when we believed. The night is far spent, the day is at hand: let us therefore cast off the works of darkness, and let us put on the armour of light" (Romans 13:11, 12).

To the Corinthian believers he wrote, "**Behold, I shew you mystery; we shall not all sleep, but we shall all be changed, in a moment in the twinkling of an eye, at the last trump: for the trumpet shall sound, and the dead shall be raised incorruptible, and we shall be changed"**

(I Corinthians 15:51, 52). Also to the Corinthian believers he wrote, "**If any man love not the Lord Jesus Christ, let him be Anathema Maranatha** (accursed at His coming)" (I Corinthians 16:22).

To the Philippian believers he wrote, "**For our conversation is in heaven: from whence also we look for the Saviour, the Lord Jesus Christ**" (Philippians 3:20).

To the Thessalonian believers he wrote, "**But of the times and the seasons, brethren, ye have no need that I write unto you. For yourselves know perfectly that the day of the Lord so cometh as a thief in the night. For when they shall say, Peace and safety; then sudden destruction cometh upon them, as travail upon a woman with child; and they shall not escape. But ye, brethren, are not in darkness, that that day should overtake you as a thief. Ye are all the children of light, and the children of the day: we are not of the night, nor of darkness. Therefore let us not sleep, as do others; but let us watch and be sober**" (I Thessalonians 5:1-6).

To Timothy he wrote, "**I give thee charge in the sight of God, who quickeneth all things, and before Christ Jesus, who before Pontius Pilate witnessed a good confession; That thou keep this commandment without spot, unrebukeable, until the appearing of our Lord Jesus Christ: Which in his times he shall shew, who is the blessed and only Potentate, the King of kings, and Lord of lords**" (I Timothy 6:13-15).

To Titus he wrote, "**Looking for that blessed hope, and the glorious appearing of the great God and our Saviour Jesus Christ; Who gave himself for us, that he might redeem us from all iniquity, and purify unto himself a peculiar people, zealous of good works**" (Titus 2:13-14).

To the Hebrew believers he wrote, "**For ye have need of patience, that, after ye have done the will of God, ye might receive the promise. For yet a little while, and he that shall come will come, and will not tarry**" (Hebrews 10:36, 37).

4. John said he would come again for he closes the canon of Sacred Scripture with these words: "**He which testifieth these things saith, Surely I come quickly. Amen. Even so, come Lord Jesus. The grace of our Lord Jesus Christ be with you all. Amen**" (Revelation 22:20, 21).

We have not the time here to dwell on the imminency of His return except to say that the signs in the Bible, in the world, in the church, and in the Jew all point to the rapid close of the age in which God has permitted us to live and serve.

People ask the question, "Will anyone be saved after Jesus comes? The answer is, "Yes." There will be people saved after the Lord Jesus has returned and taken His bride to be with Himself.

However, before anyone becomes too hopeful about this, let us see who those people are who will be saved. The Bible plainly teaches that there will be 144,000 Jews saved during the tribulation—12,000 from each of the twelve tribe of Israel. There are groups today who claim to be the 144,000, but such claims are too ridiculous and absurd for us to devote any time toward refuting them. In Revelation 7:4 we read, "**And I heard the number of them which were sealed: and there were sealed an hundred and forty and four thousand of all the tribes of the children of Israel**" (Revelation 7:4). Here we plainly see that this group which are saved in the tribulation are Israelites only.

Now there is another group saved in the tribulation also. We read of them in the seventh chapter of Revelation. John said, "**After this I** beheld, and, lo, a great multitude, which no man could number, of all nations, and kindreds, and people, and tongues, stood before the throne and before the Lamb, clothed with white robes, and palms in their hands And cried with a loud voice, saying, Salvation to our God which sitteth upon the throne, and unto the Lamb. And all the angels stood round about the throne, and about the elders and the four beasts, and fell before the throne on their faces, and worshipped God, Saying, Amen Blessing, and glory, and wisdom, and thanksgiving, and honor, an power, and might, be unto our God for ever and ever. Amen. And one of the elders answered, saying unto me, What are these which a arrayed in white robes? and whence came they? And I said unto him, Sir, thou knowest. And he said to me, These are they which came out o great tribulation, and have washed their robes, and made them white the blood of the Lamb"** (Revelation 7:9-14).

We cannot afford to be too dogmatic as to the identity of this group except to say that they are Gentiles. Some Bible students believe that they are people who never heard the gospel before the rapture and were preached to by the Jew who were saved during the tribulation. This seems to me to be the reasonable and practical interpretation of this passage. There is no reason to believe that any man or woman living today who has heard the Word of God and has had a chance to be saved and refused to accept Christ will ever be saved after Jesus comes again. It means simply this —the people of our generation whom we fail to win will be forever lost in Hell with never, no never, a chance to repent, believe and be saved. As far as our generation is concerned, it is now or never!

During the first year of my Christian life, I heard a gifted man speak on the subject of the second coming of Christ. The power of God was upon him as he preached. He did not deal in technicalities; he blew the trumpet on the fact that Jesus would return to earth suddenly, unexpectedly and without further warning.

He showed from the Scripture how that only the saved would be raptured at His coming. He stirred my heart, and I became burdened about my loved ones who were lost. I spent sleepless night and troublesome days. I had horrible thoughts of Jesus' coming at any moment and taking me up and leaving my lost loved ones behind never to be seen again. I wept many tears; I prayed more than I had ever prayed before. I began to write letters back to my loved ones, friends, and acquaintances. I sent tracts in the mail and gave them out on the streets. I began to preach with new fervor and power. People began to be saved including members of my family. It has been twenty-three years ago since I heard that sermon on the second coming, and I still feel the influence of it in my life to this very moment.

I have buried several of my relatives during these twenty-three years, but not one died out of Christ. Yes, Jesus is coming! He may come today. Is there someone on your heart today who is lost in sin and without God and without hope in the world whom you might have won if you had been more concerned? **"Now then we are ambassadors for Christ, as though God did beseech you by us, be ye reconciled to God."**

III. THE BREVITY OF LIFE MAKES SOUL WINNING URGENT

The Word of God gives much emphasis to the brevity of human life. God says that our lives are like the grass of the field. It is green in the morning and withered in the evening. Our lives are like the vapor on the window, fragile and temporary, here for a moment, then gone forever. Our lives are pictured in the Bible as fleeting shadows and as a tale which is quickly told.

We Christians need to remember that from the time we make our entrance upon the stage of life until we make our exit on the other side is but a moment compared to eternity. If your life is to count for God and His cause, then you must start now. It is no wonder that David prayed, **"So teach us to number our days that we may apply our hearts unto wisdom."**

If you do not start now to win souls as a student in school, it is doubtful if you will win them when your training is finished and you are out m your chosen field of endeavor.

My own father was saved only last year. He is in his 69th year. I have prayed for him for more than twenty-three years and have travelled thousands of miles to see him and tell him of the love of Jesus.

A few months ago my heart became so burdened that I felt that nothing could be so important as the salvation of his soul. I was holding a revival in Ohio some months ago and such a burden came upon me as I have never experienced before. I made reservation by plane to go to him fifteen hundred miles away. God saved his soul and the providential leading of God in the matter was one of the greatest joys of all my life.

Some years ago I was bringing a series of sermons to a seminar in the state of Texas. After one of the services, a young man can to me and said, "Brother Tom, I am so discouraged, won't you please pray for me? I have five children, and going to school has been great difficulty to me. It looks as if I will have to give up my training and go back to secular work. I am studying for the ministry, but can't see my way through."

We prayed together and talked together for several days, and I sought to encourage him to never give up and to walk with God at any cost. Several years passed, and I heard no more from the young man until one day I read a notice that he had started a church in a needy section of the city of Houston, Texas, where my father lives. As I witnessed to my father in his home some months ago, it occurred to me to call this young man and see if his church was near my father's home. To my surprise and joy, I found that his church was only a few minutes away. I said to him, "Brother Lovell, would you come over here to my father's home and help me to lead him to Jesus."
He came over to the house, and he came burdened. He came with the power of God on Him, he came with a passion for souls. Standing out on the lawn, with the neighbors looking on, he and I led my father to a saving knowledge of Jesus Christ. How glad I am that I went to that school in Texas and preached a few years ago! How glad I am that I prayed for that young preacher boy and his wife and five children! How glad I am that he didn't quit, that he wouldn't give up. How glad I am that God led him years later to the great city of Houston, Texas, to start an independent soul-winning church.

Some of you have loved ones scattered all over the country. You say, "How can I reach them?" You ask, "How will I ever win them? Win the sinner closest to you, win him now; and the day may come when he will in turn win some one dearer to you than your own life.

I have had many people sit in the Emmanuel Baptist Church and hear the gospel and not get saved and die within a few hours afterward "**And as it is appointed unto men once to die, but after this the judgment**" (Hebrews 9:27).

IV. THE CERTAINTY OF HEAVENLY REWARDS COMPELS US TO WIN THE LOST

God promises to reward the soul winner. We shall be rewarded here in this life with unspeakable joy and in the life to come with an eternal crown. "**And many of them that sleep in the dust of the earth shall awake, some to everlasting life, and some to shame and everlasting contempt. And they that be wise shall shine as the brightness of the firmament; and they that turn many to righteousness as the stars for ever and ever**" (Daniel 12:2, 3).

Paul was tremendously concerned about this reward. He wrote to the Thessalonians and said, "**For what is our hope, or joy, or crown of rejoicing? Are not even ye in the presence of our Lord Jesus Christ at his coming? For ye are our glory and joy**" (I Thessalonians 2:19, 20); and to the Philippian believers he wrote, "**Therefore, my brethren dearly beloved and longed for, my joy and crown, so stand fast in the Lord, my dearly beloved**" (Philippians 4:1).

The great need of the hour is a crusade of gospel preaching around the world. The crying need of the hour is a revival of personal soul winning on the part of every believer. The other day I visited the home of a woman in the city of Pontiac. The woman is nearly eighty years of age. She said to me as we sat and talked in her home, "Mr. Malone, if I live till this coming October, I will be eighty years old."

I asked her, "Dear lady, are you a Christian?"

She replied, "No, Mr. Malone, I'm not a Christian. I've never been saved. In fact," she said, "I have not been to church one time since I was very young. I have reared a large family; my children are all married. I never took them to church, and I never taught them anything about the Lord, for I didn't know Him myself." She continued, "You don't know how lonely I am. Nearly thirty years ago my husband died, and for thirty years I've lived alone. You don't know how lonely it is living all alone like this," she said as her eyes filled with tears.

I said to her, "Thank God, you need not be alone. You can have a Friend Who sticketh closer than a brother. You can have One Who will walk with you and talk with you, and One Who will call you His own forever."

I had the joy to take my New Testament from my pocket, give her the gospel, and lead her to a saving knowledge of Jesus Christ.

Then, I felt led to ask her this question, "Dear lady, has anyone ever taken the Word of God and explained to you how to be a Christian, bow to be saved as I have done today?"

She looked at me and answered, "No, Mr. Malone. I'm nearly eighty years old, but I can truthfully say that in all my life, in nearly eighty years, no one ever took the time to speak to me about my soul or to explain to me how to be saved." After the woman had been led to the Lord and prayed the sinner's prayer, my heart filled with joy. I walked out of her home and standing on her porch, I looked less than sixty feet across the street. There stood a fundamental, Bible-believing, church. I thought, "In God's Name, how could it be possible that one could live just across the street from a church of so-called Bible-believing, fundamental, soul-winning people, and never one time be spoken to about her soul and no effort be made to win her to the Lord?"

Jesus said, "**Go unto all the world and preach the gospel to ever creature**." Many times I think we as Christians, in a backslidden condition, are the greatest enemy the gospel ever had. God help us to send the gospel and to win the lost until Jesus comes.

I think of two sisters, one saved and the other lost. One went bed early one evening with her Bible in her arms. She was reading it before going to sleep while her older sister was dressing for an evening of gaiety and frivolity in the world. As the older sister stood before the mirror dressing, she put a beautiful broach in her hair. The broach sparkled with many jewels. She said to her Christian sister who was lying in bed hugging her Bible to her bosom and enjoying her faith in Jesus, "Why don't you dress as I do? Why don't you enjoy the things I do? Imagine the admiration I will get from this one piece of jewelry alone as I dance tonight to the tune of the orchestra on the dance floor."

The Christian sister, lying in bed hugging her Bible to her boson replied, "I am trying to win people to Jesus, and I have won some. Someday I will wear a crown that will outshine ten million flaming suns."

That is true, dear friends. I would to God this very hour that somehow or another God could get in the hearts of every one of us the importance of the saving of men's lives from eternal fire. That is the most important thing. Nothing else in the world is as important.

CHAPTER THREE THE HOLY SPIRIT

TEXT: "... **there standeth one among you, whom ye know not**" (John 1:26).

READ JOHN 1:15-30

In this first chapter of John we read, "... **there standeth one among you, whom ye know not.**" We know that this verse speaks of Jesus Christ. It was prophesied in the Old Testament that John would come as a forerunner of Jesus. The Bible says that before Jesus would be born as a babe in Bethlehem there would come another great character who would preach with great power, great crowds would hear him, he would be like a voice in the wilderness. John and his ministry fulfilled these Old Testament passages. Now when the people came to John and said, "*Are you Christ or is He yet to come? Are you the One of whom the prophets in the Old Testament spake concerning One Who Would come as the Saviour of the world?*" John replied, "**I am not he.**" Then he said this, "***There standeth one among you whom ye know not. He has come; He has been in your midst; you have heard Him speak; you have seen Him perform miracles; you have watched Him at work, and yet you do not know Him.***"

Now John spake this of the Lord Jesus Christ, the Son of God. I want to change the meaning of that text a little bit today. I shall no do injury to the truth; I shall do it very reverently, and, I believe, with the Holy Spirit of God leading. I want us to take that statement today, "... **there standeth one among you, whom ye know not**," and apply it to the Holy Spirit of God.

There was no excuse for people not to know Jesus when He came! The Bible had given much detail about how He would come, when He would come, and where He would be born, and what would attend his ministry. There was absolutely no excuse for the people in Jesus' day not to recognize Him and know that He was the Christ of God, the Saviour of the world. But they didn't. John was truthful when he said, "... **there standeth one among you, whom ye know not.**"

The same Bible tells us how the Holy Spirit would come, when He would come, what He would do, the miracle signs and wonders that would attend His coming. Yet, my friends, there are so many people today who do not actually know in a real, vital, wonderful way that blessed member of the trinity, the Holy Spirit of God.

Now I will tell you why I know that what I am saying today is necessary and important and why we should give thought to it. Ever year on a day called Good Friday (and there is nothing said in the Bible about it) we observe the death on the cross of the Lord Jesus Christ! For three hours the stores close, for three hours the radio stations give time to councils of churches and ministerial groups; and all over the world people commemorate the death of Jesus on the cross one day out of the year. There are some things about it, of course, that are unscriptural. Every day we should thank God that Jesus died, but we say so much of Calvary and of the day He died, Good Friday so- called. Three days later we observe what we call Easter, and of all the days in the year that is the day when the highest number of people in the fifty-two weeks out of the year attend the house of God, the day we observe the resurrection of Jesus Christ. There are three things that the New Testament is taken up with: the death of Jesus on the cross the resurrection of Jesus from the grave, and the coming into the world of the Holy Spirit of God.

We have our Good Fridays, we have our Easters, but to show you the low standard of Christianity and the lack of knowledge on the part of many people about the coming and ministry and work of the Holy Spirit I ask you, "How often have you heard of believers observing the anniversary of Pentecost?" How little emphasis is given today to the fact that the Holy Spirit of God came into the world on the day of Pentecost, baptized believers into the body of Christ and dwells in this body until this very hour. ". . . **there standeth one among you whom ye know not**."

I do not know of any subject I could speak on today or any subject we could think about on which there is more misunderstanding than the work of the Holy Spirit of God. There is much misunderstanding about Him; for instance, some people refer to Him as an "It." They think of Him merely as an influence. Let me tell you, do you know this morning if you are a child of God that the Holy Spirit is with you and He is in your body. The Holy Spirit is a real Person, just as real as Jesus, just as real as God the Father.

The Bible tells us of all His wonderful characteristics. He walks; He loves; He can be grieved; He can be quenched. You can't grieve an influence. You can't grieve an object. You can only grieve a person.

Mrs. Malone came home from a service some months ago and told me this wonderful story. I have thought of it many times since she told it to me. She said she heard a preacher tell this story of something that happened in the life of a man and his wife. This woman had a mental illness. She had been to doctors and she had been in hospitals. They had done everything in the world they could for her. Finally, the doctor said to the husband, "I know of but one thing else that I want you to do. I want you to take your wife back to the house where she was before she got sick. I want you to take her walking in the garden like she used to walk. I want you to have her in the very surroundings where she used to be. I want you to do as nearly as you can the very things that you did together before she got sick."

The man took her back to the old home place. They walked in the surroundings, the yard and the old familiar scenes and out in the garden. One day as they walked together in the garden holding hands, she gripped his hand and all of a sudden looked at him and said, "Why, you are here."

"Oh yes," he replied, "I am here."

She asked, "Where have you been?"

"Why, Darling, I have been by your side all the time. I've never left you; I've never forsaken you; I have been right with you every moment, but you just didn't realize my presence."

She could hardly believe that there was one who had not left her for a moment. How true this is of the Holy Spirit. Maybe your heart is saying this morning, "Where is He? Where is He?" If you are a Christian, He is by your side. The Bible says, "**What? know ye not**

that your body is the temple of the Holy Ghost which is in you, which ye have of God, and ye are not your own? For ye are bought with price." The Holy Spirit is with every Christian.

You say, "But I am not a very good Christian." I don't feel that I am either, and you feel that you are, that shows you are not. You say, "I am not very old Christian; I'm not a very strong Christian." The Bible does not teach that the Holy Spirit dwells with just the strong and mature, but the Bible teaches that the Holy Spirit makes His abode in the bodies of every single child of God, young or old, weak or strong.

The fullness of the Holy Spirit is another thing, and usefulness in the hands of the Holy Spirit is another thing, but the indwelling Presence of the Holy Spirit is something that is a possession of every Christian in this room today.

There are a lot of folks who misunderstand about the Holy Spirit. There are people, a lot of good people, who read into the Bible some things that the Bible does not teach. On the other hand, there are many wonderful truths concerning the outworking of the Holy Spirit through us which are so sadly ignored. This probably accounts for the fact that so many preachers, so many Christians, and so many churches are not seeing people saved today and are not getting the job done.

The more I read the Bible, the more I study the great commission to the Church, the more time I spend in prayer and meditation about this matter of the fullness of the Holy Spirit and His endue-ment and power, the more I believe that the primary and fundament reason that God gives the fullness and power of the Holy Spirit is that people might win souls to Jesus Christ. Some covet this fullness and power, they say, that they might speak in tongues. Others covet this power that they might be joyful and happy and sometimes very noisy and generous with their "Amens" and "Hallelujahs."

The early church got the job done and was successful in church evangelism because they were Spirit-empowered for soul winning. Some covet the power of the Spirit, they say, in order to heal the sick.

I believe that God can heal the sick in answer to prayer, but to magnify "healing" above the "Healer," the Lord Jesus, is not the result of the fullness of the Holy Spirit.

You know people get all excited and all concerned and they start to saying that the work of the Holy Spirit is something that the Bible does not teach that it is at all.

Here is the most wonderful thing to me about the Holy Spirit in the life of a Christian. Jesus said, **"Howbeit when he, the Spirit of truth, is come . . . he shall not speak of himself . . . He shall glorify me.**" If you want to know where there is a Christian who is full of the Holy Spirit, you find a Christian who is magnifying and exalting and lifting up the Lord Jesus Christ, and you will find one full of the Holy Spirit. If you want to find a church that is full of the Holy Spirit, find one that is making Jesus known to sinners who are lost and without God. I wouldn't give you a nickel for a so-called Spirit-filled life that never won a soul to Christ.

You know it is so easy to get off on the wrong track on the ministry of the Holy Spirit. There are a number of symbols in the Bible which typify the Holy Spirit. I believe that a practical approach to the interpretation of these types of the Holy Spirit will help us toward an intelligent under-standing of the work of the Holy Spirit in and through the believer. Every important work of the Holy Spirit is prefigured in the types and symbols which refer to Him.

I. THE HOLY SPIRIT AS A FIRE

The Holy Spirit is a fire. In Acts 2 the Bible says that when the Holy Spirit came, He came symbolized by fire. In the Old Testament you remember that when God called the Children of Israel out of bondage and set them on their way to the land of Canaan, God told them they were going to need divine leadership more than human leadership. God told them He would lead them by night by a pillar of fire in the heavens. That fire in the heavens was symbolical of the Holy Spirit of God. Fire does a number of things.

Fire refines. There is nothing in the world that will clean a dirty piece of metal like a refining fire.

Fire warms. Thank God that where the Holy Spirit is there is a warmth. *Fire illuminates.* The Holy Spirit of God illuminates.
Fire does something else. Fire cleanses.

There is nothing in the world that will clean a Christian so much as the fullness of the Holy Spirit of God. Yonder in the city of London years ago when the Black Plague was killing literally thousands of people, those people asked, "How are we ever going to stop all this disease?" They did not know as much about medicine as medical science knows today. People were dying. The black plague was spreading and killing people everywhere. They didn't know how in the world to stop it. Do you know the thing that actually stopped it? One day there took place a great fire like the Chicago fire, and that fire swept through the most diseased part of that city and stopped the black plague. I don't know a thing in the World that will arrest and put an end to worldliness and uncleanness and sin in the life of a Christian like getting down on his knees and confessing his sin and praying through the Holy Spirit that indwells his body and emptying himself and asking the Holy Spirit to come in all His fulness and all of His refining power and sweep out all the things that grieve the Lord Jesus Christ. Do you know Him as a fire?

A careful study of the word "fire" as it is used in the Word of; God will show it symbolizes a number of wonderful things.

For instance, when Moses saw the bush on fire at the back side of the desert, it no doubt symbolized the presence of God, and Moses was told, "**Put off thy shoes from off thy feet, for the place whereon thou standest is holy ground**" (Exodus 3:5). Fire, as it is sometimes used in the Bible no doubt speaks of the Lord's approval or good pleasure. When God approved of His mighty prophet Elijah as he challenged; the modernistic preachers of wicked Ahab, we read, "**Then the fire of the Lord fell . . .**" (I Kings 18:38). Fire in the Old Testament evidently spoke of God's protection, for God said of Israel, "**I will be unto her a wall of fire round about**" (Zechariah 2:5). God will give to the Spirit-filled winner of souls His wonderful Presence, His approval; and blessing and His protection as we take the gospel to the ends of the earth.

John said, **"There standeth one among you whom ye know not."** Do you know the blessed Holy Spirit as a cleansing, warming, illuminating, directing and convicting fire?

II. THE HOLY SPIRIT AS WATER

Do you know Him as water? The Bible speaks of Him as water. Now notice something. John 7:37-39 reads: "**In the last day, that great day of the feast, Jesus stood and cried, saying, If any man thirst, let him come unto me, and drink. He that believeth on me, as the scripture hath said, out of his belly shall flow rivers of living water. (But this spake he of the Spirit, which they that believe on him should receive: for the Holy Ghost was not yet given; because that Jesus was not yet glorified.)**" Here is the ministry of the Holy Spirit in the life of a believer. It is like an artesian well—the out-flowing, the fruitful life, the reaching, the blessing, the touching of others for God.

A week or two ago Mrs. Malone and I saw something that we have thought of a good many times. I never saw anything more wonderful. In a meeting down in Detroit in a church pastored by one of our seminar students, there was a seventy-year-old lady, stone blind, who couldn't walk as you and I can, who couldn't get in that door unless somebody helped her, who could not find a seat unless somebody led her. In one week in one small church, she brought ninety-five people who had never been before—a blind woman.

That woman lived in an apartment building. Down below her was an apartment; up above her was an apartment; on this side was a neighbor; on that side was a neighbor; across the street in front was a neighbor; across the street in back was neighbor, and in one night she had every last one of them in the house of God.

She said, "I want to introduce you to my neighbor that lives on this side; I want to introduce you to my neighbor that lives on that side; I want to introduce you to my neighbor that lives upstairs; I want to introduce you to my neighbor that lives downstairs." She brought ninety- five people in one week, and we beg people who have been saved twenty years to get one person in the house of God.

Stone blind! Do you know why many a Christian can't influence anybody? They don't have the outflowing life. They live in their own little world. They live for "me and my home and my family" and let the rest of the world go to hell!

When I saw that woman, who was staring off into space stand and present eighteen people that she had in one service when I was there, I said, "***Oh God, I am not worthy to have two good eyes; I'm not worthy to have two good hands, a strong pair of legs and a healthy body. I don't feel worthy of it, and if You will help me, dear God, I am going to reach people for Jesus Christ***." Let me tell you, if a blind woman with the outflowing of the Holy Spirit of God can reach ninety- five people in seven days, don't you sit in this audience and say, "I can't reach anybody or I can't win any souls to Jesus." Do you know the Holy Spirit as water? "**There standeth one among you, whom ye know not**."

III. THE HOLY SPIRIT AS A RUSHING WIND

Do you know the Holy Spirit as a rushing wind? On the day of Pentecost there came a mighty rushing wind. That speaks of His power, the power of the Holy Spirit of God. I will say this here and now, there is no power for a Christian to win souls except by the breath of God, the Holy Spirit. Jesus very plainly taught that the work of regeneration in the human heart is only accomplished by the power of the Holy Spirit. Jesus said, "**The wind bloweth where it will, and thou hearest the sound thereof, but knowest not whence it cometh, and whither it goeth: so is everyone that is born of the spirit**" (John 3:8). Just as the wind is powerful, invisible and immaterial so is the wonderful work of the Holy Spirit in regeneration.

I have seen that wonderful power come upon humble people with little or no speaking ability. You know Moses tried to get out of accepting a job of leadership from God on the grounds that he was a poor speaker. God met this frail excuse by promising to send Aaron; along with Moses to do the talking. Aaron went along all right, but when

Moses got on fire for God, he had no trouble with his speaking and Aaron rarely ever got a chance to say a word! You do not have to have the "gift of gab" or be an expert conversationalist in order to be a soul winner. Some of the best soul winners I have ever known were actually very timid people.

I have seen that power come upon people of little or no education! I have actually known a few of the dear saints of God along the way who could barely read and write and who never made a public speech or sang a solo but who were great soul winners because of the power of the Spirit of God in their lives.

I have seen that wonderful power come upon people with little or no talent. Talent is a wonderful thing, but I sometimes think its importance is very much over played. Consecrated talent is a wonderful thing, but I learned long ago that if we wait to get talented people to do the work of God, we may never get the job done. I have known some very talented and capable people who did not win souls and seemed to have no compassion, no tears, and no broken heart.

Give me the man or woman clothed upon with that mighty power which filled the upper room where the one hundred and twenty prayed and it will be incidental with me whether or not they are talented or handsome! God wants the glory to belong to Him and He wants people to know that it is not by human might or power but by His Spirit. He sometimes chooses very weak and uncomely vessels to bear His gospel to the ends of the earth. Oh, my friend, covet the best gift! Be sure you are energized and motivated by the blessed Holy Spirit.

The Holy Spirit is also symbolized in the Bible by oil. He is set forth in Ephesians 1:13 as a seal, but I wish to pass over these in order to emphasize the work of the Holy Spirit as symbolized in the Word of God as a dove.

"There standeth one among you, whom ye know not."

IV. THE HOLY SPIRIT AS A HEAVENLY DOVE

Do you know Him as a dove? When the Lord Jesus was baptized in the river Jordan, the Holy Spirit came upon Him in the form of a dove. There is a lot that can be said about this. A dove is the purest animal in the world.

- A dove never has but one mate. A dove will die before she will ever be untrue to her mate.
- A dove is a mournful bird; it rarely sings a happy song. It broods.
- The dove is a symbol of peace.

Noah sent a dove and a raven out of the ark. The raven never came back, for out there were the old decayed bodies and all the filth of a world destroyed with the flood. That satisfied him that he never came back. The clean little dove went out the window to an olive tree, picked off an olive branch which speaks of peace and came back into the ark. The Holy Spirit in the life of a believer speaks of love, of brooding over the souls of men, of a pure life. The Holy Spirit is with you today; He is in your heart if you are a Christian.

Sometime ago I read of a Christian lady on a boat who was alone as far as anyone could see. There was a would-be attacker on that boat that would rob her and bother her. He stood at a distance as the boat cruised on the Hudson River in New York and he watched her. Just before she got off the boat, he said to her, "Are you alone or do you have a companion?"

She replied, "I am not alone; I have a companion."

The boat docked and she walked off the boat and went down the street. This would-be attacker followed her a few feet behind. Finally, she came to the door of her home and reached in her purse and took out the key to open the door. He rushed up as if he would rob and harm her and said. "You told me a lie. You said you had a companion and you were not alone. You lied to me."

She smiled as she said, "I didn't lie to you. I told you I was not alone but that I had a companion."

He said, "I don't see anybody."

"I know you don't," she said, "because you are blind. You can't see Him. You see, Sir, I am a Christian; I am saved; and since the day that the sweet Holy Spirit of God came into my heart, I have never been alone."

She unlocked the door and went in as he muttered something like, "I don't want that kind of company," and went on his way.

I'm not alone, thank God, and I never will be for right here in this body of mine lives the Holy Spirit.

Do you know Him today as a burning flame, an ever flowing well, a mighty rushing wind? "**There standeth one among you, whom ye know not**."

CHAPTER FOUR WHAT HAPPENED ON THE DAY OF PENTECOST?

TEXT: "**And they were all amazed, and were in doubt, saying one to another, What meaneth this?**" (Acts 2:12)

It is my desire today to speak to you on the subject, "What Happened on the Day of Pentecost?" The Scripture is found in Acts, Chapter 2. The text is in the form of a question in verse 12, ". . . **what meaneth this?**"

Let me say in the very beginning of a discussion of this very delicate, but most important subject, that in dealing with any Bible doctrine one's motives and one's heart and mind should be baptized by love for all the believers of God, whether or not they agree with our interpretation of God's Holy Word. I do think, by God's grace and through His infinite mercy, I am able to speak with a kind disposition toward all of the Lord's people, the saints in Christ Jesus everywhere.

This message is not designed to harm, but to help. It is not designed to ridicule, but to reveal the truth of God as the Lord has given it to us. We make no claim to having all the answers, but we do claim to be a student of the Bible which we have read through many, many times in more than twenty years of study. We do claim to have the Holy Spirit in our heart and life. He is our Teacher. We do claim that we have surrendered to that Holy Spirit and that our bodies have become the temple of His dwelling place. We do believe that the Spirit of God can lead us as a servant of the Lord in the proper accurate interpretation of the Word of God.

Many times the people of God allow prejudice and tradition and other things to taint or interfere in their interpretation of God's Holy Word. There can be no doubt whatever but that the Holy Spirit works through human agency in soul winning. God uses men to win men and women and young people to a saving knowledge of Jesus Christ. There can be no true Scriptural evangelism apart from the ministry and power and conviction of the blessed Holy Spirit. There can be no spiritual power apart from Him, for Jesus said, "**But ye shall receive power after that the Holy Ghost is come upon you** . . ." (Acts 1:8). There never has been a great soul winner who did not give a sane and practical and scriptural emphasis to the ministry and Person of the Holy Spirit. Many have misunderstood the manner and purpose of His coming into the world on the day of Pentecost. May God give us receptive hearts, hearing ears, seeing eyes to understand what actually happened on the Day of Pentecost.

I. WHAT DID NOT HAPPEN

Now first, let us notice four things which did not happen.

A. The Holy Spirit Did Not Come in Answer to Prayer

The Holy Spirit of God did not come on the Day of Pentecost in answer to prayer, which is so commonly taught and commonly believed. How well do I know that one hundred twenty people for a period of ten days were in an upper room in prayer and in one accord. Following this ten-day prayer meeting the Holy Spirit came, but did He come because they prayed? My answer is, "No."

You remember Jesus said in John 16, ". . . **it is expedient for you that I go away: for if I go not away, the Comforter will not come unto you; but if I depart, I will send him unto you. And when he is come, he will reprove the world of sin, and of righteousness, and of judgment: Of sin, because they believe not on me; Of righteousness, because I go to my Father, and ye see me no more; Of judgment, because the prince of this world is judged.**" Notice carefully, Jesus said, ". . . **it is expedient for you that I go away: for if I go not away, the Comforter will not come unto you; but if I depart, I will send him unto you.**"

I would like to ask you, friends, this question, "Would Jesus have broken His word if the disciples had not prayed?" He said, "**I will send him unto you.**" If Jesus had not sent the Holy Spirit, the Lord Jesus would have gone back on His word. His promise was not contingent upon the prayers of the people of God in the upper room. The Holy Spirit would have come on the Day of Pentecost in answer to promise rather than in answer to prayer. He would have come had the disciples not uttered a prayer in the upper room. He did not come in answer to prayer. He came in answer to promise.

In a sense He came in answer to prayer, but it was the prayer of Jesus and not the prayer of the one hundred twenty in the upper room. Jesus said, "**I will pray the Father, and He shall give you another Comforter, that he may abide with you forever**" (John 14:16).

Now you might say, "Brother Tom, why this technicality?" Simply this, there are many of God's dear people, my brothers and sisters in the Lord, whom I love and with whom I could have sweet fellowship on many, many truths taught in God's Word, who are teaching and practicing that a Christian must pray that he might receive the Holy Ghost after he is saved.

The Bible does not teach that.

The Holy Spirit does not come into one's life in answer to prayer after he is converted. The Holy Spirit comes into one's life when he is saved, and one cannot be saved without His incoming. Jesus taught this to Nicodemus when He said, "**Except ye be born of water, and of the spirit, you cannot see the kingdom of God**" (John 3:5).

Paul wrote to the believers at Corinth saying,

"**What? Know ye not that your body is the temple of the Holy Ghost which is in you, which ye have of God and you are not your own? For ye are bought with a price: therefore glorify God in your body, and in your spirit, which are God's**" (I Corinthians 6:19-20).

So you see that the Bible teaches that every believer, young or old, weak or strong, taught or untaught has the presence of the Holy Spirit.
The important thing to consider, however, is this question, "Does the Holy Spirit have you?" Does He possess you and fill you? Does He control your entire being, thoughts, words, activities and every phase of your life? For you to have the Holy Spirit is one thing and for Him to have you is another. We do need to pray for His fulness and power.

Jesus said, "**If ye then, being evil, know how to give good gifts unto your children: How much more shall your heavenly Father give the Holy Spirit to them that ask him** " (Luke 11:13). It does not take God long to do the filling after we have done the emptying. No, I say again that we are not to pray for His incoming; we already have that, but we need to wait and tarry and pray for His fullness and enduement for effective witnessing for Christ.

B. They Did Not Speak in the Unknown Tongue

Now, notice the second thing that did not happen on the Day of Pentecost. Many people will not take the time to read and see whether or not my words are true. They with a biased mind and a prejudice heart, will say, "Mr. Malone does not believe all the Bible." But contend that the early church did not speak in an unknown tongue on the Day of Pentecost.

I have on my desk now several letters, one in particular, which reads like this, "Brother Malone, why do you not believe all the Bible? Why do you not believe that the Holy Ghost came upon the disciples and they spake in the unknown tongue as an evidence of the power of the Holy Ghost in the second chapter of the book of Acts?"

I do not believe that because it is not taught. There is nothing taught in the second chapter of the book of Acts which deals with the Day of Pentecost on the subject of the unknown tongue. A careful reading of these first fourteen verses in Chapter 2 of the book of Act shows some sixteen different nationalities of foreign-born Jews.

Verse 8 reads, "**And how hear we every man in our own tongue,** (or language) **wherein we were born?**" They did not say, "How hear w every man in an unknown tongue?" They said, "**And how hear we ever man in our own tongue**," or dialect, or language. This, beyond any shadow of a doubt, speaks of their native language and does not refer to an unknown tongue.

God wrought a miracle through the power o the Holy Spirit. These sixteen different nationalities of foreign-born Jews heard in their own native language the wonderful Word of God as preached by the spirit-endowed and anointed Simon Peter and the understood exactly what he said. It is the unknown tongue which listed in I Corinthians as one of the nine gifts of the Spirit.

Now let us be fair, let us be honest. The unknown tongue as evidence of the presence of the Holy Spirit in the life of a believer is definitely not taught in the second chapter of the book of Acts which deals with the Day of Pentecost particularly.

C. This Chapter Does Not Teach That All Visible Manifestation of That Particular Day Are to be Repeated.

Now in the third place, the second chapter of the book of Acts does not teach that all the visible manifestations of that particular day were to be duplicated and repeated in the body of Christ in the days to come.

For instance, the Holy Spirit came on the Day of Pentecost in two manifestations, one of which was visible and the other audible. The visible was the cloven tongues of fire. Now it would be absurd and ridiculous to say that we could expect to see today visible cloven tongues of fire coming upon the people of God who were anointed and endowed with the power of the Holy Spirit of God. It would also be ridiculous to say that we hear a mighty rushing wind.

Fire in the Bible is often used as a symbol of the cleansing effect of the Holy Spirit, and wind is used as a symbol of His life-giving, life-breathing effect and of His mighty power to move upon people. So we cannot teach and be true to the Scriptures that all that happened on the Day of Pentecost must be duplicated. However, let me say that God uses clean tools in His work. We need today as much as ever before the cleansing and refining effect of His presence and fullness.

D. The Pentecostal Experience Did Not Immediately Affect Gentiles

In the fourth place; something that did not happen on the day of Pentecost was an immediate effect upon the Gentiles. Remember, in the second chapter of the book of Acts the Holy Spirit came only upon the Jews, and the Gentiles were not immediately included.

Consider the fact that the body of Christ, of which every believer is an important part, is made up of both Jews and Gentiles, mostly Gentiles, who have been born again by the Spirit of God. This second chapter of the books of Acts is an experience which relates particularly to the Jews, but afterwards has its effect upon the Gentile.

II. WHAT DID HAPPEN

Like those in Jerusalem who came and saw this great demonstration let us ask the question, ". . . **What meaneth this?**"

Then may the Holy Spirit of God give us the answer from His Holy Word, not from tradition, not from ecclesiastical doctrine, not from human experience alone, but from the Bible itself. ". . . **What meaneth this?**"

What actually happened on the Day of Pentecost?

A. The Scriptures Were Fulfilled

In the book of Joel, Chapter 2, verses 28-32 we find the wonderful Promise of the coming of the Holy Spirit into the world. Joel prophesied or wrote under inspiration about 800 years before the birth of Christ. So 800 years before the Day of Pentecost it was promised through the Prophetic Scriptures that the Holy Spirit of God would come into the world. Read very carefully these verses in the second chapter of the book of Joel. Notice two or three outstanding things. First of all, the Holy Spirit was to come in the last days. Verse 28 reads, "**And it shall come to pass afterward.**" "**Afterward,**" we are told by Bible scholars, means in the last days. There is no question about this. The proper interpretation of the verse is "***And it shall come to pass in last days.***"

Many times people say to preachers, "Preacher, do you believe that we are in the last days?" There is no question about that. The last days started on the Day of Pentecost. We have been in the last days for nearly two millenniums. This is the age of the Gentiles. This is the last dispensation before the coming of Jesus. The next dispensation is the millennium. These, beyond any question, are the last days. We have been in this particular period in the history of the world for over 1,900 years.

This prophetical passage in the book of Joel tells us two things about these last days, or this age of the church.

First, it tells us how it will begin. It is written that it would begin with an outpouring of the Holy Spirit, which took place and was fulfilled on the Day of Pentecost.

Second, it tells us how it will end. It will end as Joel said, with ". . . **wonders in the heavens and in the earth, blood, and fire, and pillars of smoke. The sun shall be turned into darkness, and the moon into blood, before the great and terrible day of the Lord come**." This shows how these last days or the age of the Gentiles or the day of the body Christ will end. It will end with the coming of the Lord Jesus to receive His church unto Himself, then, after seven years, with a visible return of the Lord with His saints in the execution of judgment and vengeance of God upon the world.

Here in one breath the prophet Joel spoke of the beginning and ending of this age in which you and I are living and witnessing for Jesus Christ. It is a very short period of time in the mind of God. If in one breath a prophet spoke of its beginning and its ending, you and I should realize as never before that the time is short. The coming the Lord draweth nigh. He shall come suddenly and quickly to receive His waiting bride. What we do for Jesus must be done quickly; and it must be done, if to be effective, in the energy and power and demonstration of the blessed Holy Spirit of God who tabernacles His deity within the confines of our bodies.

B. Types Were Fulfilled

In the second place, types were fulfilled. We mean by this that the Old Testament prophesied in type the Day of Pentecost. Read very carefully Leviticus, Chapter 23. In this chapter seven great religious feasts or festivals are listed and explained which were observed by the Jews under law in the Old Testament. We will notice carefully these seven feasts.

First of all was the Feast of the Passover, which *represents Christ our Redeemer or our passover.*

Second was the Feast of Unleavened Bread, which *speaks of communion on the part of the redeemed with the Redeemer or the fellowship of a believer with his Lord.*

Third was the Feast of Firstfruits, which is *typical of the resurrection of Christ.*

Fourth was the Feast of Pentecost, which is *typical of the descent of the Holy Spirit to form the church and baptize believers into the body of Christ.*

Fifth was the Feast of Trumpets, which has a prophetical significance for it *speaks of the gathering of the Jews from all parts of the earth to the land of Palestine.* This is going on today and prophecy is being fulfilled!

Sixth was the Feast of Atonement, which *represents the repentance of the Jews and their national conversion.*

Seventh was the Feast of Tabernacles, which *represents, of course, the millennium and also the kingdom rest for Israel and for all the redeemed.*

Let us go back now and see the third and fourth of these seven religious feasts, which are the Feast of Firstfruits and the Feast of Pentecost. The Feast of Firstfruits, as we have said, represents the resurrection of Christ. In Leviticus 23:15 we read, "**And ye shall count unto you from the morrow after the sabbath, from the day that ye brought the sheaf of the wave offering; seven sabbaths shall be complete: Even unto the morrow after the seventh sabbath shall ye number fifty days.**"

Now notice, God plainly said that between these two feasts would be fifty days, starting on Sunday or the morrow after the Sabbath and then count seven sabbaths which would be forty-nine days, and then on the morrow after the seventh, as it is clearly set forth, which is a period of fifty days between the feast representing the resurrection and that representing Pentecost. How beautiful and minutely accurate was the fulfillment of this. The Lord Jesus Christ the Bible says appeared to His own some twelve distinct times during a period of forty days after His resurrection. Then after ten days of prayer in the upper room, the Holy Spirit came on the Day of Pentecost just exactly as He was typically prophesied in the 23rd chapter Leviticus in Old Testament types.

The Day of Pentecost was a fulfillment of Old Testament types. How marvelous and beautiful is the structure of God's Word!

C. Promise of Jesus Realized

The promise of Jesus was brought to fulfillment on the Day of Pentecost. As we have already mentioned, the Lord Jesus on more than one occasion promised that the Holy Spirit would come after His ascent back through the heavens to the right hand of the Father.

The are three great facts taken up in the New Testament — the appearance of Jesus the first time to redeem, the coming of the Holy Spirit into the world on the Day of Pentecost to baptize believers and to form the body of Christ, and the coming again into the world of the Lord Jesus Christ to receive His own unto Himself. How wonderful is God's Word. How accurately its promises are fulfilled.

The promise of Jesus was realized on the Day of Pentecost. He had kept His word.

- How it must have thrilled the hearts of these believers.
- How it must have strengthened their faith.
- How it must have edified and built them up in a holy reverence for God and His Word and a holy fear of such a sovereign, mighty God.

No wonder they went out filled to overflowing to witness and to win people by the thousands as they did.

D. Holy Spirit Baptized Individual Believers

In the fourth place the Scriptures teach that the Holy Spirit baptized individual believers into one body, not into an organization, but into an organism, a living body as it is taught in the Bible.

In I Corinthians 12:13 we read, "**For by one Spirit are we all baptized into one body, whether we be Jews or Gentiles whether we be bond or free; and have been all made to drink into one Spirit. For the body is not one member, but many**." Then in verse 20, "**But now are they many members, yet but one body**." This body was formed on the Day of Pentecost as Paul clearly teaches in his Corinthian epistle.

III. WHAT MAY CONTINUE TO HAPPEN

We have now seen briefly what did not happen and what did happen. Let us now see what may continue to happen as a result Pentecost.

A. Every Christian Can Have the Fullness of the Holy Spirit

Let us be clear that a Christian has the Holy Spirit. If he did not have the Holy Spirit, he would not be a child of God. Jesus taught that one must be "**born of the spirit**." Paul taught that "**if any man have not the Spirit of Christ, he is none of his**." To have the Holy Spirit is one thing and to let the Holy Spirit have you is another.

A lady came very excitedly to a minister friend of mine who is a godly man and a soul-winner and a great student of the Scriptures and said to him, "Oh, praise God, I have the Holy Spirit."

He said, "I want you to know that there is one thing better now."

"Oh," she said, "What could be better than having the Holy Spirit?"

My preacher friend replied, "That the Holy Spirit may also have all of you."

We sometimes have been accused of not believing in the anointing and the power and the demonstration of the Holy Spirit. How untrue this is. We do not seek to interpret the Word of God by experiences of others or by the doctrines of certain ecclesiastical organizations or by the traditions of men. We want to be true to the Scriptures, but we do believe with all our hearts in the anointing and the power of the Holy Spirit of God as the Bible teaches.

In Ephesians 1:13 we are taught, ". . . **ye were sealed with the Holy Spirit of promise**," which means God has placed His seal of ownership upon us and the presence of the Holy Spirit in our lives means we belong to God and He belongs to us and we have been recipients of an eternal life imparted through the Spirit.

Also in Ephesians 4:30 we are told, "**And grieve not the Holy Spirit of God, whereby ye are sealed unto the day of redemption**."

You see, dear friends, the Holy Spirit is more than in influence. He is a person. The Bible attributes to Him the characteristics and attributes of a person, and being a Holy Spirit He can be grieved with anything unholy in the life of a Christian.

Then in Ephesians 5:18 we have the plain command, ". . . **be filled with the Spirit**." This is a command of God to every believer. Oh, how we believe in this. How we daily pray as we confess sin and empty ourselves of all that which is unclean and contrary to His will and His Word. We pray daily that we might be filled to overflowing with the Presence of that blessed Person of the trinity, the Holy Spirit that out of our lives might run an endless, constant river of blessing, an o flow of His inward work.

In I John 2:20 we read, "**But ye have an unction** (or anointing) **from the Holy One, and ye know all things**."

Yes, we believe the Bible teaches a special anointing of the Holy Spirit for Christian service, for soul-winning, for cleansing, for separation, for power to be all that God would have us to be.

There is only one incoming of the Holy Spirit, but there may be many uprisings or fillings of the Holy Spirit. Every time a Christian by repentance and confession is willing to empty himself, God is certainly willing to fill him to overflowing with the presence of the Spirit of God.

B. Continual Power to Win Souls

In Acts 1:8 we read, **"But ye shall receive power, after that the Holy Ghost is come upon you: and ye shall be witnesses unto me both Jerusalem, and in all Judea, and in Samaria, and unto the uttermost part of the earth."**

Here the Lord Jesus plainly teaches the result of power of the Holy Spirit in and upon the life of a believer. It is that he might be a witness unto the Lord.

The early church started at home. They started in Jerusalem. Acts 5:42 we read, **"And daily in the temple, and in every house, they ceased not to teach and preach Jesus Christ."** They went two by two which is the Bible way. They started at home, and they went from house to house.

After Jerusalem, the city, they went into Judea, the province. After that province, they went into Samaria and then to the uttermost parts of the earth. This is God's program. The Christian who talks about the power of the Holy Spirit and claims some definite work of the Spirit of God in his life and does not win souls to the Lord Jesus Christ is speaking of an experience which is contrary to the Word of God and the teaching of Jesus. The Holy Spirit is given in power upon the lives of God's people that they might be witnesses unto Him. We have no confidence whatever in the Christianity of people who make loud praise to God in public but have no witness and no testimony in the shop, store and above all in their home in the midst of their families. The Holy Spirit is given to win souls to Jesus Christ. Oh, may God give us a hunger and thirst for the fulness of the Holy Spirit that we may take the gospel to the ends of the earth that multitudes may hear and believe and be saved.

C. Souls Can Be Saved Anywhere

The third thing that can happen as a result of Pentecost is that people can be saved anywhere and everywhere that they will call in repentance and faith upon the name of the Lord Jesus Christ.

Remember that in the book of Joel, Chapter 2, verses 28-32, which deal with the coming of the Holy Spirit on the Day of Pentecost, one of the results prophesied was, "**And it shall come to pass, that whosoever shall call on the name of the Lord shall be delivered**."

Now then, Simon Peter, on the Day of Pentecost, in preaching that sermon so greatly blessed of God mentioned this prophecy and quoted it again. In Acts 2:21 he said, "**And it shall come to pass, that whosoever shall call on the name of the Lord shall be saved**."

Thank God the Holy Spirit is omnipresent. He is where you are now. He is able to speak to your heart to convict you of your need and to point you to the Lamb of God Who died in your stead on the cross of Calvary and bore in His body on the tree all your sins and mine.

Thank God, as a result of the coming of the Holy Spirit, wherever you are—on a sickbed, in a prison cell, at the bedside in your home, in the church, anywhere—you can call upon the Lord Jesus Christ and trust in His atoning blood and you can be saved. May God help you to do it today.

CHAPTER FIVE WHY MANY CHURCHES OF AMERICA ARE DEAD AND FORSAKEN

TEXT: "**Why is the house of God forsaken?**" (Nehemiah 13:11).

Two of the most wonderful books in the Bible for the Christian worker are the books of Ezra and Nehemiah. The book of Nehemiah especially sets forth some essentials for success in the Lord's work. If the fundamental methods used by this spiritual giant Nehemiah were to be used by Christians and New Testament Churches today, we would see great revivals and multitudes saved. The book of Nehemiah should be taught in every course on soul winning and evangelism.

The Word of God had come to pass with such minute and wonderful accuracy. The Children of Israel had been taken into captivity for a period of 70 years as God said they would be. At the close of the 70 years captivity after the Jews had been scattered to the various heathen nations, God began to work in the hearts of men like Ezra and Nehemiah. The Temple of God in Jerusalem so ruthlessly destroyed by the cruel and wicked Nebuchadnezzar must be rebuilt. The walls of the glorious city of Zion lay in shameful debris. Who would dare to undertake such a gigantic task? Who would have the courage in face of such bitter and persistent opposition to take a little chosen handful of believers and assail such a tremendous problem? Only a God-called, Spirit-empowered, giant-hearted man such as Nehemiah!

What a wonderful man is this man Nehemiah. He has so many admirable characteristics of leadership. He was a man of prayer, and the book of Nehemiah records his prayers and how earnestly he prayed. He was a man of compassion; he wept over the pitiful condition of the city of Jerusalem and the people of God. He was a humble man, a man who knew the weaknesses and the sin of his own heart, for he confessed that he himself as well as his fellow countrymen had sinned. This shows his humility. He was a man of courage, and he needed great courage for every subtle effort of the

Devil was used to dishearten him. Notice how this opposition manifested itself. The Devil works the same today to keep churches and preachers and laymen from winning souls and getting the job done.

1. *The enemies were grieved because there was a small group of people with deep concern for the work of God.* "**It grieved them exceedingly that there was come a man to seek the welfare of the children of Israel**" (Nehemiah 2:10).

- *The enemies laughed at this God-called minority*: "**They laugh us to scorn and despised us and said, What is this thing that you do?**" (Nehemiah 2:19).

- *The enemies ridiculed and counted this true and scriptural work a small and insignificant matter.* They said, "**Even that which the build, if a fox go up, he shall even break down their stone wall**" (Nehemiah 4:3).

- *The enemies joined hands and cooperated together to defeat this true work of God.* "**And conspired all of them together to come and fight against Jerusalem and to hinder it**" (Nehemiah 4:8).

- *The enemies sought to bring about an unequal and unscriptural union of believers and unbelievers.* They said, "**Come, let us meet together in some one of the villages**" (Nehemiah 6:2) and Nehemiah sent them this classic answer, "**I am doing a great work, so that I cannot come down: why should the work cease, while I leave it and come down to you?**" (Nehemiah 6:3).

- *The enemies tried to frighten them by threatening words.* They said, "**Their hands shall be weakened from their work, that it be not done**" (Nehemiah 6:9). Nehemiah responded with this compassionate prayer, "**Now therefore, O God, strengthen my hands**" (Nehemiah 6:9).

Because the few remained courageous and true, a great work was done, a great revival broke out, and great honor was brought upon the Lord and his work.

There are some things recorded in the book of Nehemiah that he did which show that he feared no one. These things he did in the power of God, for there is no other way that a man could get by with some of the things that he did except it be done in the energy of the Spirit and by the power of God. For instance, he threatened the merchants who desecrated the Sabbath Day and sold their wares in the city of Jerusalem on the Holy Day. He said, "**If you do so again, I will lay hands on you.**" He showed courage when he went into the temple and threw the furniture of one wicked Tobiah out of the holy chamber in the temple. He showed courage again when he pronounced a curse upon the backslidden, vacillating Jews who had married wives of Ashdod. He threatened them, pronounced a curse upon them and smote certain ones and plucked out their hair. Then we read that he chased the son-in-law of Sanballat — chased him away, ran him off. He was a man of great courage. He was a great worker and great leader. There is much to be learned about Christian leadership and soul winning and church building in the book of Nehemiah. In many respects, it is a book on how to work for the Lord.

We read what the enemy will do when we undertake to work for God. The enemy tried to make fun of what they were doing and laugh them out of their holy purpose. They stood back and said, "**If a fox were to go upon the wall, it would break down**." Then they threatened them and told them they were violating the law of the King and of Persia and that they would suffer for it. Thus they tried to put fear in their heart. Then they tried to join them.

The Devil has never changed in his tactics.

He seeks to laugh us out of our work; he seeks to put fear in our heart as to the consequences of being true to God; he seeks to get us to join the wrong crowd or allow them to join us in order to weaken the forces of the church. What a wonderful book it is.

I am concerned primarily in this message with the statement found in the last chapter of the book which is a most vital and important question, "**Why is the house of God forsaken?**"

In this chapter there are five reasons shown why the house of God in

Jerusalem was forsaken. I want to make it clear that the house of God can be forsaken in more ways than by one's physical presence. We are seeing in many instances today thousands of people attending the house of the Lord, and yet the house of God, the true, scriptural house of God and the work of God is being forsaken. It is being forsaken in the very same five ways that this chapter points out that the house of God was forsaken in the days of Nehemiah. Thousands of churches across America today know nothing about the old-fashioned prayer meetings. The Sunday night evangelistic service has long since been abandoned by many. A soul-winning visitation program is unheard of in most churches. God's house has been forsaken!

I. THE HOUSE OF GOD WAS FORSAKEN BECAUSE OF A LACK OF SEPARATION

First of all, the house of God was forsaken by lack of separation. In the first three verses in this 13th Chapter of Nehemiah we read this significant statement: "**On that day they read in the book of Moses in the audience of the people**" (They were reading from the first few verses of the 23rd Chapter of the book of Deuteronomy).

Reading these verses they discovered that God had said many years previous that the Ammonite and Moabite should never come into the congregation of God forever. Now Nehemiah finds that the Ammonite and the Moabite, these heathen, unconverted ones, were in the congregation of God and were allowed there. The thing that caused them to see this lack of separation was the reading of the Word of God.

You know, dear friends, it is most important today that we know what the Bible says on the subject of separation. There is much involved. The Christian individually is to be separated from evil and from the world and from all that is anti-Christian and anti-God. The church collectively as a body is to be a separated group. We are to be separate doctrinally as well as from the standpoint of conduct. Many today who are separated from the standpoint of Christian conduct are not separated from the standpoint of Christian doctrine; that is, the very freely mix and mingle with people who do not believe in the virgin birth of Christ and the entire verbal inspiration of the Word of God, and many other cardinal truths held dear by the born again child of God. We must be careful that we are not only separated from the standpoint of Christian doctrine, but separate also from the standpoint of Christian conduct and vice versa. One without the other is not complete consecration. The Pharisees were separated from the standpoint of conduct; that is, they lived a self-righteous life; but from the standpoint of Christian doctrine, they were not separated.

The substituted the traditions of men and their own conveniences and that which was expedient for them for that which was clearly set forth and laid down in the Word of the eternal God. These Ammonite and Moabites and all their descendants were people upon whom the curse of God had rested. Ammon and Moab were the two sons born to the two wicked daughters of Lot by their own father after the destruction of Sodom and Gomorrah. The curse of God was upon them; yet they had been allowed in the house of the Lord.

Then we read in verse 3 of this chapter of a "**mixed multitude**." Mark that phrase in your Bible. It is found a number of times. In Exodus 12:38 we read of a "**mixed multitude**" who went out of Egypt when Israel was redeemed by blood. This mixed multitude went along, not because they had been redeemed and sheltered and cleansed by the blood of the Passover lamb but because they had seen God work miracles in Egypt. They went along from a fleshly standpoint, from the standpoint of curiosity, and to be with a great group of people who were going out. Their hearts were not changed.

Later on, hundreds of years later, we find this mixed multitude still present approximately 1000 years after they went out of Egypt. We find also in the book of Numbers, Chapter 11, verse 4 that when Moses was leading the Children of Israel out of the bondage of Egypt to the freedom and blessings of the land of Canaan and had come to Kadesh-Barnea, a most important place and most epochal event in the life of Israel, that this same "**mixed multitude**" was there to hinder and caused a weeping and murmuring among the people of God.

The mixed multitude is always a hindrance. It always has been and always will be. There is absolutely no point to be gained by the admission of unconverted people into the membership of churches. In fact, it is a wicked sin against God. God's Word says: "**Be not unequally yoked together with unbelievers**." God says in His book. "**Come out from among them and be ye separate and touch not the unclean thing**." The greatest need in the churches of America today if they are to be soul winning churches is to get back to the Bible in the matter of Christian separation.

II. THE HOUSE OF GOD WAS FORSAKEN BECAUSE OF THE LACK OF CLEANNESS

We find in verses 4-9 of this 13th Chapter of Nehemiah that Eliashib, the priest, had taken a compromising attitude toward Tobiah, a wicked man who had opposed the work of the Lord carried on by Nehemiah and his faithful cohorts. We read how this priest with great compromise had allowed Tobiah to occupy a most important and sacred chamber there in the temple. Tobiah had taken up his abode there. This is most important because this chamber typically speaking was a chamber reserved for the Lord Jesus Christ. There the meat offerings and frankincense were stored which were typical of Jesus.

Actually, it was a room which spoke of His glorious Person; but Tobiah, an enemy of the work of God, had been allowed into the Holy Temple and into this most sacred spot which was to be occupied typically by the Person of our Lord Jesus Christ. We read how Nehemiah came to Jerusalem and was grieved in his heart because of this compromise and uncleanness in the house of the Lord.

He went into this particular chamber in the temple and threw all the furniture of wicked Tobiah out into the street and commanded that the chamber be cleansed, and it was. This speaks of cleanness in the house of the Lord. God's church is always to be a clean church. The Bible tells us how that God through the Holy Spirit from time to time has purged out and cleansed wickedness from the midst of the people of God and that purging and chastising on the part of God has always brought fear to the hearts of unbelievers and caused them to be converted and to respect and revere God.

This was true in the days of the early church as recorded in Acts 5 as God struck with sudden death Ananias and Sapphira, who lived a life of pretense and sham and pretended to have achieved a level of spirituality which actually they did not possess, There were funerals and sudden death in the midst of the early church because God wants a clean church.

I read years ago of one of the bloody revolutions that took place in France during the reign of King Louis XVII and his beautiful queen Marie Antoinette. History tells us of how the little Prince, Louis often called The Little Dolphin, was a most feminine looking little boy with beautiful curly hair. Some even hinted that the little Prince was feeble-minded. The revolutionists took the King and Queen and executed them. Just before they were to take the life of The Little Dolphin, the wicked crowd suggested that they have some sport and jest with him.

They said, "Let us not kill him now; let us take him down in the slums and filthy parts of the city and turn him over to old Aunt Mag, the most wicked and vile woman who ever lived. This they did. Aunt Mag, it is said, used all kind of vulgar and vile language in the presence of the Little Prince. She set before him vile and corrupt food and urged him to eat. She sought to induce him to do things that were corrupt and vile. It is said that the Little Prince would shake his curly locks and clinch his little fist and beat upon the table and cry, "I will not; I will not. Don't you know I am the son of a King? I shall not defile myself with these wicked thoughts and this vile and corrupt food. I'm a child of a King. I'm a child of a King." He said, "You may kill me, but I will gladly die before I will defile myself with these wicked things."

This ought to be the spirit dominating the heart and life of every Christian. First of all we should realize we are children of the King. We are not our own; we have been bought with a price. We thank God that because of the new birth and the cleansing blood and the indwelling Holy Spirit we are a royal people. God give us the spirit to say, "Gladly would die before I would defile myself and desecrate my body, which is the temple of the Holy Ghost." The house of God is often forsaken in the matter of cleanness on the part of the members of the household of faith. Only clean Christians will ever be able to win the lost and check the awful flood tide of wickedness which threatens to destroy our homes and churches and freedom.

III. THE HOUSE OF GOD WAS FORSAKEN BY LACK OF GIVING

Verses 10-14 show how the tithe had ceased to be brought into the temple, and as a result of this the priests were not even being supported and had gone back to the fields and farms in order to make their living. Now the Word of God teaches that His work is to be supported by the tithes and offerings of the Lord's people. There is no argument on the subject.

There is no question whatever but that the Bible teaches this is God's way and the only way God has ordained in the Scriptures that the work of the Lord be supported. All manner of excuses can be given why people do not tithe. Some say, "I believe tithing was under law, and I am at complete liberty under grace to do as I will on this matter." I will show you, God helping me, that the Bible does not teach that tithing was at first instituted under law. Abraham in Genesis 14 tithed. This was at least 500 years before the law was given at Sinai. Abraham tithed before the law was given, and God commended him for it.

We read further in Genesis 28 that Jacob made a covenant with God. He said, "**If God will be with me, and will keep me in this way that I go, and will give me bread to eat, and raiment to put on, So that I come again to my father's house in peace; then shall the Lord be my God . . . and of all that thou shalt give me I will surely give the tenth unto thee.**"

Jacob tithed some several hundred years before the law was ever given. So the tithe was not instituted under law; it was reaffirmed under the Mosaic Law. Malachi 3:10 is certainly a tremendous statement concerning the tithe and its connection with the house of God. Malachi 3:10 reads, "**Bring ye all the tithes into the storehouse, that there may be meat in mine house, and prove me now herewith, saith the Lord of hosts, if I will not open you the windows of heaven, and pour you out a blessing, that there shall**

not be room enough to receive it."

It is a significant thing that the tithe in the Bible is connected with the house of God. It is our conviction that God wants the Christian to give to the local church if that local church is truly the house of God in a scriptural sense. In fact, referring again to the instance of Jacob and his tithe we find even in this case that the tithe is connected to God's house, for when Jacob made this holy resolve and covenant with God to tithe, he poured oil upon a stone and called that place Bethel. Bethel means *the house of God.*

The story has been told of a young man years ago during the days of great depression who was forced to leave his father's home to seek to make a living for his own. This young man as he left his father's home was passing a farmer's house, and the farmer came out and took him by the hand and said, "Bill, you are leaving your father's home and going to the city. There are two or three words of advice I would like to give you. First, be a Christian; serve God and never forget that you belong to Jesus. Second, the first dollar that you ever make and all that God gives you in your life, be sure to honor God with at least a tenth."

The young man looked in the face of the Christian farmer and replied, "These two things I will observe." He went into the city and he gave 10 cents of the first dollar he made unto the Lord. He followed this practice throughout all of his career.

That man was William Colgate, who was the head of the Colgate industries and out of whose hands have come hundreds of thousands of dollars for the work of God. It pays to tithe because it pays to obey God, and it is always best to observe the Word of the Lord. Many times the house of God is forsaken by people's not giving of their tithe and offering unto the Lord.

God will not bless a Christian and give him a soul-winning ministry if he is disobedient to God in the matter of the tithe and offering, and God will not bless a church and make it a great soul-winning church if it attempts to support the gospel in any other way except by the scriptural method of the tithe and offering.

IV. THE HOUSE OF GOD WAS FORSAKEN BY THE DESECRATION OF THE SABBATH DAY

In verses 15-22 we read that Nehemiah was grieved because of the merchants who came to the walls on the Sabbath Day and were allowed to peddle their merchandise and sell their wares to the people in the city and go through the opened gates on the Sabbath Day. This, of course, was a flagrant violation of the Holy Scriptures. The people of Israel had the seventh day, the Sabbath Day, set aside as a holy day unto the Lord, and they were not to pick up sticks or cook food or go out of their tents, much less to be peddling merchandise on the Sabbath Day.

Now understand that the Bible speaks plainly that the Sabbath was given not to the church, not to the saved gentile, but the Sabbath was given is the book of Exodus clearly points out unto Israel. In Exodus 31:13 God said, "**Speak thou also unto the children of Israel, saying, Verily my sabbath ye shall keep: for it is a sign between me and you throughout your generations; that ye may know that I am the Lord that doth sanctify you**."

Now the Lord never gave the seventh day to the church. If I had no other proof that the Lord's Day is the day that we worship and meet together in the house of God than the fact that it is the day that Jesus arose from the grave, that would be enough. However, the Bible goes further. Acts 20:7 records the observance of communion in the early church on the Lord's Day, not the seventh day. I Corinthians 16 tells us that we are to bring our tithe unto the Lord on that day, and we are to forsake not the assembling of ourselves together in the house of the Lord bringing our offering with us on the first day of the week.

Now then, in spite of the fact we do not keep the seventh day or the Sabbath, we observe the first day of the week, the Lord's Day; and in spite of the fact that there is a distinct difference between the two, one was a day of complete rest and inactivity for Israel while the other is a day of worship and meeting together and service for the Lord for the church. The Lord's Day is a holy day. We believe that it is wrong to violate the holy day of the Lord and not to observe and keep it. It certainly is wicked for a Christian to absent himself from the house of the Lord on the day of the Lord. Desecration of the Sabbath Day was a sin in Nehemiah's generation. Forsaking the house of the Lord on the Lord's Day is a sin in our day which is prominent among hundreds of thousands of professing Christians.

In the interests of the nation we must keep the Sabbath. Said the great Victorian statesman, W. E. Gladstone, "Tell me what the young men of England are doing on Sunday, and I will tell you what the future of England will be." For our own sake, for the sake of our families, our sons and daughters, and all coming after, let us safeguard the Sabbath Day. The Christian Sabbath has been provided for us in the wisdom of God for our physical, mental, and spiritual well-being, and we act wisely when we use this God-given day in the worship and service of our Maker, and in giving heed to the things that matter most.

A few years ago the ladies of my church told me this strange and yet true story. These ladies said they went out to the woods hunting some kind of berries. While they were walking out through the woods along a little road, they suddenly heard an awful noise. They looked in the direction of the noise, and it appeared that a building had collapsed. They went over to the building and there stood a man shaking like a leaf. The color had left his face, and he looked deathly sick. He said to these ladies, "Just a few seconds before this garage fell, one of my little children who was playing in there came out. Then the garage collapsed into the pile of rubbish that you see now. I am a Christian, but I let God's house go, and I got out of fellowship with God, and I stayed away from the Lord and built this garage on the Lord's Day. Look at it now." He continued, "Just think, but for the mercy of God my little child would have been crushed beneath that heap of stone and wood at this very minute."

I'll tell you, my friends, when God says something in His Word, I believe that it is important, God says, ". . . **forsake not the assembling of yourselves together as the manner of some is**." David said in Psalm 122: "**I was glad when they said unto me, Let us go into the house of the Lord**." A Christian is always connected with the house of God.

Now there are 52 Sundays in the year. In our section of the country there are at least ten Sundays in the winter that some fellow who doesn't really want to serve God will say, "Well, it's just too cold." There are at least ten Sundays in the summer, around July and August, when he will say, "Well, it's just too hot."

It's not too hot to go to the grocery store, not too hot to go to work, but too hot to go to church. It's too cold ten Sundays and it's too hot ten Sundays. There are at least ten Sundays when it is pouring down rain. Now wouldn't it be awful, friends, for a Christian to get a little bit damp going to the house of God? Wouldn't that be a tragedy? You know, I have played ball in the rain, and it never bothered me a bit; I've gone hunting in the rain, and it never hurt me a bit. There are ten Sundays that it is too wet to go; this makes thirty Sundays. There are six Sundays when it snows too much.

Some old boy from Tennessee looks out the window and sees the snow. His feet hit the cold floor, and he says, "The Lord is leading me to stay home today." This makes thirty-six Sundays. Now there are five Sundays out of the year that you have company. Let me tell you, company soon learns whom they can visit on the Lord's Day and get a good meal and not be asked to go to the house of God. If your relatives and your neighbors know that they can come to your home and with the slightest excuse you will refrain from going to the house of God, you will never win them to Jesus. They have no confidence whatever in your testimony. Five Sundays you have company. Oh, don't embarrass them. It would be an awful thing even to suggest that they go to the house of God.

You know, nobody bothers me on the Lord's Day. I have never had a caller on Sunday morning. Never. People know who is going to the house of God. Yes, five Sundays you have company. Then there are five Sundays that you have to return the visit. You say, "I've got to go visit Aunty Molly and Uncle Joe. They are getting old." You never do this on Saturday, or Monday, or Tuesday, or Wednesday, or Thursday, or Friday. It must be on the Lord's Day.

Then there are four Sundays that you are sick. Actually one day you are sick; the other three you think you are. Johnny sneezes on Friday so all six members of the family stay home on the Lord's Day. That takes up fifty Sundays, which leaves two. You very piously say, "I'm going to church today." That is Easter. Again you say, "I'm going to church today." That is Christmas.

That is a sorry kind of Christianity, isn't it?

You laugh about it, but I want to tell you if you as a Christian, and Tom Malone as a preacher have come to the place that we accept that kind of Christianity, there is something wrong with us, and we are backslidden and not very close to God.

V. THE HOUSE OF GOD WAS FORSAKEN BY UNSCRIPTURAL MARRIAGES ON THE PART OF THE CHILDREN OF GOD

Verses 23-27 give us the pitiful record of the intermarriage of the Jews with the heathen women of the Ammonites and the Moabites, who followed the false religion of Ashdod. The pitiful results are set forth, for the Bible tells us their children were confused and mixed up. They spake half in the speech of Ashdod and could not speak in the Jew's language because of the mixed marriage and intermingling on the part of God's people and the heathen people.

Mixed marriages and unscriptural marriages always cause disaster and confusion.

- Children are misled and confused.
- Homes are broken ending in divorce.
- Souls are sent to hell.
- The Word of God is violated.
- The Spirit of God is grieved.
- The house of the Lord is hindered.
- The work of God is hindered as it was in this instance.

No wonder Nehemiah was so stirred up on this matter he contended with them, pronounced a curse on them, smote certain of them and pulled out their hair. He demonstrated that he was opposed to this violation of the Word of God.

I remember years ago hearing a very Spirit-filled and wonderful evangelist tell of a family he knew in the East when he was a young preacher. It was another case of a young Christian woman who stepped out of the will of God and violated the Scripture and married an unsaved man.

The young man became very successful in business and finally they became very wealthy people. The Lord blessed them with a little baby girl. She was torn between two opinions, those of her mother who sought to serve the Lord and those of her father who lived only for this world and what he could get out of it. When she reached the age of sixteen, her father bought her an automobile, beautiful clothes and sought to shove her on to the dance floor and into the mad whirl of a godless society.

When she was twenty-one, she contracted pneumonia while attending a dance. She soon lay upon her death bed. It is said that the broken-hearted mother stood on one side and the broken-hearted father stood on the other side.

The father came and brought the jewels, the keys to the beautiful car, some of the evening clothes and laid them on the foot of the bed and sought to comfort the daughter's heart in her dying hour. The daughter, it is said, looked at her father and in her dying moments said, "Father, none of these things mean anything to me now. What I have needed all along is my mother's Saviour. You've led me astray. You've led me wrong. You've damned my soul. I'm dying now, and there is no hope."

In a moment she closed her eyes in the silent sleep of death and departed this life without hope and went out to meet God totally unprepared. It never pays to violate God's Holy Word to live in sin and unbelief.

Why is the house of God forsaken? Why have you forsaken the Lord? Why have you turned from Him? Why have you failed to trust Him?

CHAPTER SIX HAVE FAITH IN GOD

TEXT: "**And Jesus answering saith unto them, Have faith in God**" (Mark 11:22).

Read Mark 11:12-26

There are a number of verses in the eleventh chapter of Mark that are closely related to prayer. Jesus said in verse 17, "**My house shall be called of all nations the house of prayer, but ye have made it a den of thieves** ." He also said in verse 23, "**Whosoever shall say unto this mountain, Be thou removed, and be thou cast into the sea; and shall not doubt in his heart, this which he saith shall come to pass; he shall have whatsoever he saith**."

You know, dear friend, that God is saying here in His Word, that you can have "**whatsoever he saith**." "**You can have whatsoever he saith**." "**What things soever ye desire, when ye pray, believe that ye receive them, and ye shall have them**" (verse 24). Jesus said you shall have what you desire if you pray in faith believing.

But these are not the texts which seem to be foremost in my mind and on my heart this morning. My text only has four words in it. They have been a great challenge to my heart for many years. I trust that they will be to yours today.

In verse 22 we read, "**And Jesus answering saith unto them, Have faith in God**." Have faith in God! It seems the Lord led us to this verse at a most appropriate time. There never has been a time in the history of the world when the individual people needed faith in God as they need it now. I doubt if there has been a time in the history of the work of the Lord when all of us needed to have faith in God, not in our ability, not in the schemes of men, but faith in God.

I am amazed when I look through the Word of God and find out the importance of faith and all that the Bible has to say about it.

In the book of Matthew, for instance, Jesus gives what we might call scale of faith. He speaks to people and says, "**What, have you no faith?**" Certainly that is the description of a large multitude of people across the face of the earth today. They have no faith, no faith whatever. They have no faith in God, no faith in Christ His Son, and no faith in His Word.

Then Jesus spoke to His disciples and several different times said to them, "**Oh, ye of little faith**." There are people with no faith at all. Then Jesus plainly taught that there are saved people whose faith is weak and who have very little faith. Jesus said on one occasion about one person, "**I have not found so great faith, no not in all of Israel**."

So here we have three things Jesus said on the subject of faith in book of Matthew — "**no faith**," "**little faith**," "**great faith**." It ought to be the heart's cry of every single one of God's children that we should have "**great faith**."

Paul in writing to the believers at Rome in Romans 14:23 said, "**Whatsoever is not of faith is sin**." It is a sin, my friend, not to have faith, strong, active, living, vital faith that draws upon the resources of God, brings the flood-tide of peace into your own soul and causes things to happen in your Christian experience.

Faith in the Bible, of course, is set forth as one of the nine fruits of the Spirit. To have faith, to be one of great faith, means to have the fulness of the Spirit, for the Bible teaches us that love, joy, peace, long suffering, gentleness, goodness, faith, meekness, and temperance are the nine fruits of the Holy Spirit. You cannot possibly have a strong faith and ignore the Holy Spirit in your life. Faith is one of fruits of the Spirit. When the Holy Spirit is allowed to possess completely and fill with His blessed fullness, our faith is going to be the kind which pleases God and gets things from His Hand.

Faith is a part of our Christian armour. Paul in writing to Ephesian church gave the description of the armour of the people of God in Chapter 6. He told that we are to be dressed up in the helmet of salvation. We are to have the breastplate of righteousness. Our loins are to be girt about with truth. We are to be men and women of prayer. We are to have our feet shod with the preparation of the gospel of peace. Our all conquering weapon is to be the living and powerful Sword of the Spirit.

Paul closes his description of the Christian's armour in Ephesians 6:16 by saying, **"Above all . . ."** Friends, Paul said, inspired of God, **"Above all, taking the shield of faith, wherewith ye shall be able to quench all the fiery darts of the wicked."**

The eleventh chapter of Hebrews is a great chapter of faith. It is the greatest thesis ever written on the subject of faith and it is written in a most beautiful language. This chapter honors the saints of all ages who have been strong in the faith. In Hebrews 11:6 God says, **"Without faith it is impossible to please God."**

The word **"faith"** is found only twice in all the Old Testament; once in Deuteronomy 32:20 where we read of a **"froward generation, children in whom is no faith,"** and again in Habakkuk 2:4 where we read, **"the just shall live by his faith."** The fact that the word **"faith"** is found only twice in the Old Testament by no means infers that there were not men and women of great faith in Old Testament times. They that pleased God and walked in holy fellowship with Him and made an impression on their generation were men of great faith in God's Person and power and promises.

I John 5:4 sets forth the importance of faith, for there we read, **"This is the victory that overcometh the world, even our faith."** It is absolutely impossible to please Almighty God and it is absolutely impossible to overcome the world without having what Jesus spoke of as **"great faith."**

I think the importance of faith is seen in a conversation Jesus had with Simon Peter, one of the twelve. One day Jesus in predicting the denial of Simon Peter said, **"Simon, behold Satan hath desired to have you that he may sift you as wheat: but I have prayed for thee that thy faith fail not: and when thou art converted** (or turned back again)**, strengthen thy brethren"** (Luke 22:31-32).

Notice these wonderful words of Jesus which have to do with our faith, **"I have prayed for thee that thy faith fail not."** The Christians of strong faith are the ones who stand true to the Word of God and win souls to Jesus Christ, and they are a comfort to the brethren.

I am so glad that Jesus said to Peter, "**I have prayed for thee that thy faith fail not**." Do you know, dear friend, that the faith of the people is so important in God's sight that yonder at God's right hand this very moment, right now Jesus is seated in the heavenlies in the presence of God, faithful to God's throne that our faith might not fail. I say unto you this moment, "**Have faith in God**." God give the church, God give you as Christian men and women and young people an unusual and extraordinary faith.

I have never been able to define faith. I could not give you a clear definition of it this morning if my life depended upon it. There is only one attempt made in all the sixty-six books of the Bible to define faith. That is the opening statement of the eleventh chapter of Hebrews where we read, "**Now faith is the substance of things hoped for, the evidence of things not seen**." This is the only attempt in all God's Word define faith.

But I know a little something about what faith means.

- Faith means believing God.
- Faith means believing God against all odds.
- Faith means seeing the unseen.

Thank God, a Christian can see by faith what no one else has ever seen except a Christian. I think of so many instances in the Bible where men saw the unseen, saw the evidence and saw the substance of things not seen. In fact, Paul said, "**We look not on things which are seen but on the things which are unseen. For the things which are seen are temporal but the things which are unseen are eternal**."

You know friends, everything you can see, including this body in which I live and the body in which your soul and spirit abide, everything you can see, every object either animate or inanimate, everything you can see with physical eye, the Word of God calls temporal. That is, it is related to time. But God tells us that with the eye of faith we can see the unseen which is related to eternal things and will live as long as God lives.

I think of the prophet Elisha and his servant when he had fled to Dothan pursued by the wicked armies of Ben-hadad, the Syrian King. There, as he looked out across the country side, he saw the great host soldiers and their mighty chariots of war. His servant trembled with fear; but as Elisha looked out, thank God, he saw something which the servant did not immediately see. He said to him, "**Don't you see what have seen?**" Though yonder are hundreds of thousands of the armies of Satan, thank God, "I see the chariots of the Lord and an army angels in chariots of fire." Faith pulls aside the curtain of obscurity and faith sees the unseen. Faith distinguishes between the spiritual and the carnal. Oh Father, give the people of God today a vision to see that which the naked eye and the unconverted eye could never look upon.

Notice what Jesus said in these four words, "**Have faith in God**," not in man. The greatest thing that ever happens to a Christian is to lose faith and confidence in the flesh. Have faith in God, not in preachers, not in deacons, not in churches, not in church members, not in Christians, not in things you can see, not in circumstances, not in the brilliance and talents of man, not in numbers, not in ecclesiastical programs! Have faith in God.

Never shall I forget hearing a preacher tell of a boat's crossing the English Channel one dark and stormy night. As the boat crossed the choppy waters and stormy channel, it is said that the winds blew and the waves rolled high like mountains. It seemed such a stormy night that it looked as if God were angry with the world. While the boat plowed its way through the storm, it is said that the people screamed with fear. Some dropped on their knees and prayed. It is said that a little girl on that boat sat as calmly, quietly, and serenely as if she were in the rocking chair of the living room of her home. Someone said to her, "Little girl, as we sail across these choppy waves and it looks as if any moment this boat will go down beneath the waves, why do you have such calmness and peace of heart?" The little girl looked at the one who inquired and replied, "I'll tell you why. The captain of this boat is my own daddy. My father has crossed this channel so many times. He has crossed it through every kind of wind and storm that blows, and I know he will reach the other side tonight." Have faith in God. I have faith today to believe that the work I am in is God's work! It can never be overthrown. God's program for this age will succeed.

You know, friends, it's as it was when Jesus said to His disciples, "**Let us go over to the other side**." I think I can see Him now, standing along the beautiful blue quiet waters of the Sea of Galilee where Mrs. Malone and I were some time ago. He lifted up that omnipotent finger that created worlds and said, "**Let us go over to the other side**." They got in the boat and started for the other side. In the midst of the sea, a storm arose. His disciples began to cry, "**Master, save us or else we perish**." Jesus arose from His sleep, lifted His head from His pillow, for He was tired with weary toil, He arose to the little deck of the boat and waved His hand across the sea and the waves lay down like little lambs at their mother's breast.

You know, Jesus has said to us as Christians, "**Let us go over to the other side**." From the place where He found us bound in chains, steeped in iniquity, lost and undone and without God, He pointed yonder to the shores of heaven and said, "**Let us go over to the other side**." "**Have faith in God**."
There are not enough demons in hell or stormy winds to blow that can sink the boat of the child of God. So I say to you in this solemn hour of the world's history, have faith in God. Have faith in God for at least four wonderful things.

I. HAVE FAITH IN ORDER TO WIN THE LOST

This is the biggest job the world has even known. You remember Jesus said, "**Because I go to My Father, greater works shall you do than these works that I have done**."

God in His Word and through His Son has challenged the church of the twentieth century to greater works than Jesus did when He walked this world two thousand years ago.

- I remember that Jesus spoke to the dead, and they lived again.

- I remember that Jesus spoke to the blind, and they came seeing.
- I remember that Jesus touched the lame and crippled, and they we made whole again.

And yet, Jesus Christ has said to me that I am to do greater works than He did. I have a job to do as a Christian We have a job to do greater than raising the dead, greater than opening the eyes of the blind and straightening out the limbs of the crippled. "**Greater works than these shall you do**." What work is that? It is the work of preaching the blessed gospel of God's infinite, wonderful grace and mercy, and winning men and women, boys and girl from the fires of hell and judgment to a saving knowledge of Jesus Christ. I'll tell you that when with God working in your life, you are used to win a soul to Jesus Christ, you have done a work that is greater than creating a world or hanging a star in the sky. Have faith for the salvation of souls.

You remember the four who brought the paralytic to Jesus—four men who wouldn't quit, four men who could not be defeated, four men in whose vocabulary the words "quit" and "defeat" could not be found. They climbed up to the roof of that little old house, tore up the roof and looked down through the opening and saw One standing down there Who could make the man whole whom they brought. They start letting him down through that hole.

I have often said of all the things described in the gospels, I think I would like to have seen that miracle more than any other. I wish I could have looked up and could have seen what Jesus saw. Jesus looked up and the thing that impressed Him was not so much the crippled man borne of four letting him down through the broken ceiling. Jesus looked up and the Bible records what impressed Jesus most. He looked up, and the Bible says, "**When he saw 'their faith' he looked down and said to the man sick with the palsy, Son thy sins be forgiven thee. Rise up and walk**."

Yes, it takes faith to win the lost. These four men were absolutely void of religious selfishness. They were saturated and absorbed with a conviction that Jesus could meet the needs of their lost and crippled neighbor. The crowd in the house at Capernaum made it difficult to get to Jesus. Their task seemed impossible, but they soon graduated from the realm of the impossible to the realm of the probable, and then, thank God, moved on into the realm of reality and got the job done.

They were no doubt laughed at, criticized, and opposed, but they could not be stopped. They represented faith, prayer, perseverance and love in cooperative soul winning. No doubt some cried, "Wait a minute, you are upsetting things. Has the board met on this project? Has it been approved by the denomination? Are you sure it will set well with the religious leaders?" They were completely unconcerned with these non-essential technicalities. They did not worry about the expense of repairing the roof or the publicity that would result from their unprecedented method.

I have seen many a Christian follow God and believe God for the salvation of souls and pray right up to the time when it seemed God would save their loved ones, and then their faith wavered and they failed to win them.

- I am preaching to people this day who carry a burdened and broken heart in your bosom year after year.
- I am preaching to women whose husbands are on their way to hell.
- I am preaching to husbands this day whose wives are lost.
- I am preaching today to some of you folks whose children are out yonder on the bleak mountainside of this world in sin, away from God and like sheep who have strayed from their shepherd.

I beg of you in God's Name, have faith in God today and don't ever let go and don't ever give up and don't ever quit praying until God has given you your family for Jesus. Have faith for the salvation of souls!

II. HAVE FAITH FOR THE UNUSUAL

The Bible tells us that faith accomplishes the unusual. Sometimes people say to me, "Mr. Malone, do you believe in miracles?"

I reply, "Yes, I do." I do not believe in miracles to the extent that I think I can do anything that Jesus, Peter, James, John or Paul did. I don't believe I can raise the dead. I don't believe there is any power in these hands of mine to heal the sick. If I could heal the sick and open the eyes of the blind, I would go all the way with God. I would take all of what Jesus said, for the same Jesus that said, "Heal the sick and cast out the demons," said, "Raise up the dead." I want you to show me a man who can raise the dead. There is not one. People who say, "I can heal the sick," but they do not raise the dead take only part of what God said. Have faith in God for the unusual and remember that the paralytic whom the four brought to Jesus had his sins forgive before he had his body healed. God is specializing today in the miracle of regeneration.

I believe in miracles. I believe that my God can do things today that all the governors and senators and congressmen and the President cannot do. The Bible teaches us that many times faith has wrought the unusual, and the lack of faith has kept the unusual from happening.

You remember that when Jesus took three of the twelve and went yonder on the mountain top where He was transfigured, Moses and Elijah appeared. There were six people on that mountain top, Jesus and five men.

When Jesus and the three came back from the mountain, Moses and Elijah did not come. But thank God, when we are once in heaven, we never leave His presence and never cease to be with Him.

Down there in the valley something was going on. Jesus and the three went down into the valley, and there were multitudes watching someone lying there writhing in the dust, a picture of the sin-cursed and lost of this world. There was a boy with twitching lips and glassy eyes. There was a boy foaming at the mouth, his limbs jerking. There he was lying unconscious with dust and sweat and blood all over him as he lay on the ground. His father was wringing his hands for that dear son. Nine disciples were standing around; nine men to whom Jesus had said, "**Go into all the world and preach and I will give ye power over demons**" (and that was what was wrong with the boy).

Here this father stood with a broken heart and wringing hands. He turned to Jesus and said, "*I brought my boy to your men. I brought my afflicted son to your mighty preachers, but they could not heal him."*

The disciples couldn't cast out the demons, and they turned to Jesus and asked, **"Why could we not cast them out?"**

Jesus looked at them and said, **"This kind,"** that's the hard kind. **"This kind,"** that's the unusual kind. **"This kind,"** that's the unexpected kind. **"This kind cometh not out except by prayers and by fasting."**

Listen, friends, with faith in God and belief in prayer, I believe you can accomplish the unusual, the extraordinary, and the unexpected! Did not Jeremiah say, **"Call upon me and I will answer thee and shew thee great and mighty things which thou knowest not of?"** No Christian shall ever come to the place when his faith is not valuable. Christians should seek to face new worlds, conquer new continents, do new miracles, work new enterprises with faith in God. We need to have our faith challenged until we lean upon God to do the unusual. We need to believe that we can build great soul-winning churches and Christ-centered schools without the help or approval of men who do not believe the Bible. Have faith in God. Have faith in God to win the lost. Have faith in God for the unusual.

III. HAVE FAITH IN GOD'S PROMISES

The book of Titus says the God that promises cannot lie. I read of Abraham at the age of a hundred and his wife at the age of ninety to whom the angel of the Lord appeared and said, ***"You will have a son and through him I will bless the world and through Him a Messiah will come."*** We read in the fourth chapter of Romans that Abraham **"staggered not at the promises of God through unbelief but was strong in faith giving glory to God, and being fully persuaded that, while he had promised, he was able also to perform"** (Romans 4:20-21). God give us a faith that can reach within this Divine Book and lay hold upon His promises, pull them into our hearts and souls, believe them, and stagger not. Have faith in God. God has promised us a number of things about this matter of soul-winning.

1. *He has promised to be with us.* "**Go ye therefore, and teach all nations, baptizing them in the name of the Father, and of the Son, and of the Holy Ghost: Teaching them to observe all things whatsoever I have commanded you: and, lo, I am with you alway, even unto the end of the world**" (Matthew 28:19-20).

2. *He has promised us that our work is an eternal one and that our fruit will abide forever.* "**Ye have not chosen me, but I have chosen you, and ordained you, that ye should go and bring forth fruit, and that your fruit should remain: that whatsoever ye shall ask of the Father in my name, he may give it you**" (John 15:16).

3. *He has promised to bless us here and hereafter.* "**Then Peter began to say unto him, Lo, we have left all, and have followed thee. And Jesus answered and said, Verily I say unto you, There is no man that hath left house, or brethren, or sisters, or father, or mother, or wife, or children, or lands, for my sake, and the gospel's, but he shall receive an hundredfold now in this time, houses, and brethren, and sisters, and mothers, and children, and lands, with persecutions; and in the world to come eternal life**" (Mark 10:28-30).

4. *He has promised to reward us at the Judgment Seat of Christ.* "**And they that be wise shall**

shine as the brightness of the firmament; and they that turn many to righteousness as the stars for ever and ever" (Daniel 12:3).

IV. HAVE FAITH IN GOD'S MERCY TO SAVE THE LOST

I say unto you in closing, God is a merciful God.

Faith and God's mercy are linked hand in hand in the Bible and never can be separated. I think of two Bible characters, one a man and the other a woman who came to Jesus and asked Him for mercy. In the eighth chapter of Matthew we have the record of a man who came to Jesus and said, "*My servant is dead. I want you to heal him.*" Jesus said, "*All right, let us go to him.*"

This man replied, "*Now wait a minute, Jesus. I am a man of authority myself. I have people all around me. I say to one, 'Go,' and he goeth; and I say to another, 'Come,' and he cometh. You don't have to go where he is. I know you, Jesus. You are a miracle-working Man. You love people. You want to meet their needs. Why don't you just say the word, and then by Thy word he shall be healed.*"

Jesus said, "*All right. Go to thy home, thy servant liveth.*"

When the man went home he found it as Jesus said. Jesus saw that man walk away and said, "**I have not found so great faith in all of Israel**." He had faith in the mercy of Jesus.

A woman came to Him one day. She said, "*My daughter is vexed of a devil. She throws herself in the fire. She needs help.*" This woman was not a Jew, she was Greek, a Syrophenician, a Gentile.

Jesus pointed to her the Word of God and said, "*I cannot do anything for you, woman. It is not meet, the Bible says, to take the children's bread* (the Jew) *and give it unto the dogs* (the Gentiles)." The gospel was not yet turned fully from the Jews, God's chosen people, to the Gentiles, the heathen nations of the world. He said, "**I cannot take the children's bread and give it unto the dogs**."

That woman looked in His face (I can see her now perhaps with tears streaming down her cheeks) with great faith in His mercy, and she cried, "**Yes, but Master, it would be all right to let the dogs eat the crumbs that fall from the children's table**." She said, "*Don't you know even when royalty eats, the dogs are entitled to the little crumbs that drop from the corner of the table.*"

Jesus said to that woman, "**Oh woman! Great is thy faith: be it unto thee even as thou wilt, and her daughter was made whole from that very hour**" (Matt. 15:28).

God is a merciful God. He delights to save the lost. He loves and weeps over this lost world today, and His heart's desire is to have sinners come unto him from all the ends of the earth. We are co-laborers together with God in this all important matter of soul-winning. God's purpose in this age is not to convert everyone but to choose out a bride for His Son, the Lord Jesus. God will not fail in this purpose. We are on the winning team, thank God. **"Have faith in God."**

CHAPTER SEVEN WHY FEW ARE SAVED, MULTITUDES ARE LOST

TEXT: "**Then said Jesus unto the twelve, Will ye also go away? Then Simon Peter answered him, Lord, to whom shall we go? Thou hast the words of eternal life**" (John 6:67, 68).

There are two heart-searching questions in John 6:67, 68. The first question is, "**Will ye also go away?**" " **Then Simon Peter answered him, Lord, to whom shall we go?**" This is the second question. We will consider these two questions today: "**Will ye also go away?**" and "**To whom shall we go?**"

Jesus performed many miracles. The greatest of them, in many ways, is recorded in the sixth chapter of the gospel of John. You will remember that the Bible tells us of certain miracles He wrought such as healing the eyes of the blind, raising the dead on three occasions, and healing the sick often. This gospel of John says, "**And many other signs truly did Jesus in the presence of his disciples, which are not written in this book: But these are written, that ye might believe that Jesus is the Christ, the Son of God; and that believing ye might have life through his name**" (John 20:30, 31).

If all the miracles Jesus did were to be written, the world itself could not contain the books thereof. No one knows how many eyes Jesus opened that were blind; no one knows how many dead Jesus raised; no one knows how many times Jesus lifted some sick person by the hand and made him well again. He wrought many miracles. There is only one miracle, however, that all four of the gospels, Matthew, Mark, Luke, and John, make a record of in detail — that is the record of the feeding of the five thousand men besides women and children. No other miracle that Jesus wrought is recorded in all four of the first New Testament books.

This miracle is related to another miracle Jesus wrought which is also recorded in the gospel of John. In the second chapter, you read of the miracle of turning the water to wine. There in that second chapter,

Jesus wrought a miracle which speaks to us of His blood that would be shed. He turned the water to wine. Here in this sixth chapter, He performs another miracle when he takes the loaves and fishes from a little lad and so multiplies that lunch that it feeds thousands of people with twelve basketfuls remaining. This miracle speaks of His broken body. Thus we have the two elements that come into prominence when we sit together at the table of the Lord.

The blood shed upon the cross for the redemption of man and cleansing from sin, and the broken body of our Lord. Chapter Six in John gives us a record of this great miracle from which there are many lessons to be learned.

I am surprised when I come to the close of the record of the miracle.

I see five thousand men with their wives and children sit upon the grassy slopes around the Sea of Galilee.

I see them behold with open eyes the greatest miracle the Son of God ever wrought. I see them eat the bread that literally came from heaven.

I see them behold a miracle before their eyes direct from the Son of God.

But at the close of this chapter, I do not find what I would expect to find. I do not find this great multitude of thousands of people falling at His feet, doing obeisance to Him and acknowledging Him. I find a strange picture at the close of this chapter. I find that the great multitude had been divided into two groups—one a very large one and one a very small one.

I see a very large group at the close of this chapter turn their backs on the Son of God and walk across those grassy slopes back to the communities and cities from which they came.
I see them turn their backs on Jesus and go away from Him. I also see thirteen lonely men stand upon those grassy slopes.

As Jesus saw that multitude walk away, He turned to those twelve men and said, "**Will ye also go away?**"

This is a picture that is set forth, dear friends, in literally dozens: of places in the Bible. God divides the world. God divides the human race into two groups. They are not two equal groups, for one is always large. The other is always small.

That was true in Noah's day when a large group was destroyed by a flood and a small group was saved by an ark.
That was true in the days of Sodom and Gomorrah when a large group was destroyed with fire and brimstone and a small group was guided by an angel out of the overthrow of God's judgment.
That was true when Jesus looked at those who knew Him during the days of His public ministry and said, "**Fear not, little flock, for it is the Father's good pleasure to give you the kingdom.**"
It was also true when Jesus said, "**Enter ye in at the strait gate: for wide is the gate, and broad is the way, that leadeth to destruction and many there be which go in thereat: Because straight is the gate, and narrow is the way, which leadeth unto life, and few there be that find it**" (Matthew 7:13, 14).

This is the case in our day; few are saved, multitudes are lost. This will be the case when the Lord Jesus shall return from heaven.

Few, comparatively speaking, will be raptured away; many shall be left behind to suffer the judgment of God. No wonder the ancient prophet Joel cried, "**Multitudes, multitudes in the valley of decision**" (Joel 3:14).

You ask, "Brother Tom, can you explain why a great multitude went away from Jesus and only a little group remained with Him?"

I think if you read carefully the sixth chapter of the gospel of John, you find several reasons why people went away from Jesus. They go away today for the same reason they went away two thousand years ago. I see the same scene today Jesus saw when with broken heart and tear-stained face, He watched the thousands go away in rejection and turned to His little school and said, "**Will ye also go away?**" These thousands, yea, millions must be evangelized.

I. THEY WENT AWAY BECAUSE OF HIS TEACHING

They went away from Jesus then and now because of His teaching. You find four things in this chapter which Jesus taught on that day which are hard for people to accept.

1. *Jesus taught that He must be sought for spiritual reasons.*

On that day Jesus looked at that multitude and said, "**You seek me not for holy reasons, but you seek me for superficial reasons.**" In verse 26 of this chapter we read, "**Jesus answered them and said, Verily, verily, I say unto you, Ye seek me, not because ye saw the miracles, but because ye did eat of the loaves, and were filled.**"

Listen, Jesus said, "*Ye seek Me not because of the miracles I've done; you seek Me not because of a spiritual need in your heart; you seek Me merely because you've seen Me feed people. You seek Me for a physical reason and not for a spiritual one.*"

Let me tell you, dear friends, when you see people in great crowds today, I would to God you would think of this and discern: "What are those crowds after?"

I believe in crowds; I believe in multitudes. It's the hunger and prayer and the cry of my soul that God would help me to preach to just as many people as possible, but I ask, "What are those crowds after?"

Are they looking for the healing of the body? If they are, that might a good reason but that is not a scriptural reason for coming to Jesus, believe in Divine healing and the miracle-working power of God the human body; but I will tell you, if one comes to Christ to get nothing but a well body, he will never get his soul saved and his sins forgiven.

"**You seek me,**" He said, "**not because of the miracle I have done but because of the bread which I gave you.**" Let me tell you, my friends, you read through the New Testament and see that the miracles which Jesus wrought brought many people after Him but very few people to Him, and the miracles "so-called" today draw multitudes after Christ but few to Jesus. "**Will ye also go away?**"

2. Jesus taught that the Father must draw men to Him.

Now notice. In this chapter Jesus tells how people can come to Him. There is but one way. In verse 44 Jesus said, "**No man come to me, except the Father which hath sent me draw him: and I will raise him up at the last day**." No one can come to Jesus except he is drawn of God. He might have his emotions moved and stirred, and I believe in emotions. We need tears and excitement in our preaching and witnessing. We need warm hearts and cool heads. How many today have cold hearts and hot heads!

I never want to be one to say "I do not believe in tears and emotions in connection with the work God." You can have your emotions stirred, and in the midst of excite ment you might have your will moved upon to come to God, but no one can come to God, Jesus said, except my Father draw him. There is only one way to come to Jesus Christ and only one holy, divine purpose for coming. That is to come to be saved and to come called of God's Holy Spirit. Any soul-winning ministry must be a Spirit-filled ministry because only the Holy Spirit can draw men to God.

3. Jesus taught that man must partake of Him to be saved.

Jesus went on with His strong teaching. In verse 53 He said, "**Verily, verily, I say unto you, except ye eat the flesh of the Son of man and drink his blood, ye have no life in you**."

Notice this. It is not what the Catholic church says it is—the doctrine of transubstantiation, the doctrine that the elements actually turn to the body and blood of Jesus when they are partaken of. We do not believe that. We do not believe that Jesus spoke literally when He said, "**Except ye eat the flesh of the Son of Man, and drink his blood, ye have no life in you**."

We believe that Jesus here is saying, that except you partake of the Son of God and He becomes a part of you and comes within you as a Person to live in your temple, your body, as your Saviour, you have no life in you. In order to be saved men must be "**partakers of Christ**" (Hebrews 3:14) and partakers of "**His divine nature**" (II Peter 1:4). "That is strong teaching, Jesus, and it might cause You to lose Your crowd." True evangelism is that which brings people to a personal Christ and not merely to a program or denomination.

4. Jesus taught that the flesh profiteth nothing but the Spirit quickeneth.

Jesus went on and in verse 63 I think He made the strongest statement that any teacher or preacher could ever make. He said, "**It is the spirit that quickeneth** (or maketh alive)**; the flesh profiteth nothing.**" Dear friends, Jesus taught that it is the Spirit of God that gives life; and without the Holy Spirit of God, the flesh and all that it can do profiteth nothing.

Man can join the church; he can be baptized; he can sit at the Lord's Table; he can carry a Bible under his arm; he can engage in religious activity, but without the Holy Spirit in his heart, the flesh profiteth nothing. "**If any man have not the Spirit of Christ, he is none of His**" (Romans 8:9).

That is the kind of preaching Jesus did. When you hear that kind of preaching and teaching, don't you say that comes from a narrow and bigoted and uneducated person because that is the kind of teaching Jesus did. Strong preaching! He said, "***Seek Me for a holy purpose. You can't come except God calls you. You must actually partake, for all the flesh is of no avail without the Spirit of God in you.***" When the crowds turned and walked away, they went away because they objected to His teaching.

There is nothing more nauseating today than to hear a lot of these "so-called" modernists. There is not anything modern about them. They are as old as the day when Satan in his serpentine form went with his subtle unbelief into the Garden of Eden to bring about the fall of the human race.
They say, "We believe in the teachings of Jesus. We do not believe in a gory, slaughter-house, bloody religion. We believe in the ethics of Jesus and the teachings of Jesus."

Let me tell you, dear friends, you want to remember that it was the Son of God who said, "**Ye must be born again.**" It was the holy, spotless Son of God Who said, "**Except you eat the flesh of the Son of Man, and drink his blood, ye have no life in you**."

Don't you say you believe in the teaching of Jesus unless you believe in salvation through the medium of the bloody cross and the Son of God nailed to it.
Don't you say you believe in the teaching of Jesus unless you believe in being born from above by the regenerating miracle of God's Holy Spirit.
Don't you say you believe in the teaching of Jesus unless you believe in a literal, bodily resurrection, an empty tomb, and an occupied throne and the coming of Jesus in the clouds of glory.

The teaching of Jesus is the strongest teaching the world has ever heard, and no teacher or preacher ever spoke any stronger than Jesus. No wonder they turned and went away. He spoke in love, but He spoke the truth.

The Bible tells us that in your generation and mine people shall "**heap to themselves teachers having itching ears**." They don't desire the truth wholeheartedly all the time. They want their ears tickled, their conscience salved, and their hearts appeased but not cleansed. So they went away.

II. THEY WENT AWAY BECAUSE OF THE FEAR OF MAN

Men go away from Jesus, in the second place, because of the fear of man. The wise man of the book of Proverbs said, "**The fear of man bringeth a snare**." I've seen that in more realms of life than in the realm of Christianity. I've seen the fear of man bring a snare in the realm of politics. I've seen men literally sell their souls, their character, and their integrity to tie on to their political coat tails people and groups of people who might elect them to office. I've seen it in the realm of business and so have you. We've seen business men literally sell their honor, their character, and their good name in order to be a success in business because they were afraid to go into conflict with those who might oppose them.

How true that is in the realm of Christianity, my dear friends. We've seen men and women sell their souls in the very pit of hell itself because they were afraid to walk with that little group of twelve while the multitude turns its back and walks away. They go away from Jesus because of the fear of man.

One of the greatest evangelists this world has ever known was a converted attorney, Charles G. Finney. No other man of his generation ever experienced the kind of revivals Charles Finney knew. Charles Finney prayed and came along at a time when there was a hunger in America, especially in the northeastern section of our country. When he would walk into the plants, the machines would stop and the workers would stand motionless and still. Many times they would fall on their faces in the factories and stores and begin to cry out to God for forgiveness. He preached with such power (Oh, how we covet such power!) that people stood in the midst of his sermons and begged him to hush. He preached with such power that hundreds and hundreds of thousands were swept into the kingdom of God in one area of our country.

It is said that at night when he would ride his horse to his place of destination, he would put his horse in the stable, pull the horse blanket about his shoulders, and there in the barn somewhere he would call on God until the sun came over the hills in the morning. Oh, with what power he preached and people were saved. While he preached one night, it is said that the Chief Justice of the State of New York came walking down the aisle. He was preaching on the text: **"No man liveth unto himself."** The Chief Justice of the State of New York realized that he was not a Christian, and for the fear of his political friends he had sold his soul into hell. He walked down the aisle that night, took the hand of Charles G. Finney, and said, "I want to be a Christian." That great man asked then if he could say a word to the audience. His hair was gray with the snow of many winters and his shoulders were bent beneath the weight of many years. He faced the audience and said to that multitude of people, "For fear of my companions-at-law, I have rejected God's Son until this late hour in life. I want to beg you, young or old, right now, no matter what the cost, no matter what people may say, be a Christian."

It is said that as he stood there with outstretched arms he became a preacher — he who had just been saved for a moment — and people began to come by the scores down all the aisles to be saved. Let me tell you, dear friend, that text is as true this morning as it ever was. "**No man liveth to himself**" and no man dieth to himself. Your life today casts an influence either for God or against Him. You today are leading someone. You lead your children; you lead your friends; you are a leader whether you want to admit it or not. You may not lead many, but you lead some. Everyone in this building is a leader, and your influence you shall face at the judgment bar of God. Let me beg you, do not go away from Jesus because of the fear of man, and do not fail in the matter of soul winning because of the fear of man.

III. THEY WENT AWAY BECAUSE OF DOUBTS AND QUESTIONS

Sometimes people go away from Jesus because of doubts and questions in their minds. The Bible tells of people who had doubts questions. Nathaniel had a doubt which originated in his head. When Nathaniel saw Jesus, he said, "**Can any good thing come out of Nazareth?**" (John 1:46).

That was not a heart doubt; that was a doubt of his mind. Jesus came and met that need as He saw Him sitting beneath a tree. He called Nathaniel and proved that a good thing, thank God, came out of Nazareth. Thank God, the Jesus we preach today is able to meet and satisfy the honest intellectual doubts of people.

We read of others. John the Baptist had a doubt, an honest doubt of the heart. John the Baptist was in prison awaiting the moment of his execution. He had been faithful to God in preaching the gospel. He sent a messenger to Jesus and asked a question because he had a question unanswered. He asked: "**Art thou He that should come or look we for another?**" (Matthew 11:3). Jesus removed his doubt by saying to the messenger, "***Go tell John the blind see, the dead are raised, the lame walk. You don't need to look for any other.***" John got his doubt settled. Jesus is the only answer today to the doubts and questions of the human heart.

Thomas had a doubt. It was an honest doubt. Thomas said, "**Except I shall see in his hands the print of the nails, and put my finger**

into the print of the nails, and thrust my hand into his side, I will not believe" (John 20:25). Whether he ever did or not, the Bible does not say, but Jesus removed his doubts as far as He had removed his sins — the distance of the east from the west.

Let me tell you, dear friend, I have a challenge today for any honest man in the world. If a man says, "I am not a Christian today because I have an intellectual doubt in my head or an honest doubt in my heart," I will tell you how that doubt can be met head- on and challenged and defeated. In John 7:17 Jesus said, " **If any man will do his will, he shall know of the doctrine whether it be of God, or whether I speak of myself** ." If you want your doubt overcome, you follow what light God has given you. If you are not a Christian, you take the step Jesus dares you to take; and if your doubts are not removed, we will never ask you to have anything else to do with it. If you are willing to do the will of God and take one step at a time. I will guarantee you God will throw light on your pathway, and God will remove every doubt from your head and from your heart. People sometimes do not come because of doubts, and they go away from Jesus. "**Will ye also go away?**"

IV. THEY WENT AWAY BECAUSE OF LOVE FOR THE WORLD

People sometimes go away from Jesus because of a love for sensual, worldly enjoyment. Oh, the hundreds of people I have met in my limited experience who will not come to Jesus because they do not want to give up sinful pleasures. I was thinking in the last few hours of a girl who came to the altar led by the hand by two well-meaning relatives, her mother and an aunt. This was a meeting where I was preaching when I was just a student in college. They brought that young girl to the front, and she was bowed with conviction. Tears streamed down her face. She was deeply moved. They said, "Her name is so and so." I called her by her name and said, "Do you want to be a Christian?"

She replied, "Yes, I do, but —."

I waited to see what the rest of the statement was, and she said, "Mr. Malone, I love to dance, and if being a Christian means to give up the dance, I'm not going to do that."

I was just a student in school, and I didn't know anything about theology (I still don't know an awful lot because theology doesn't meet the needs of people's hearts, friends, but the Word of God does). I said to her, "You'll never be a Christian until you are willing to turn from the dance floor."

You ask, "Do you mean, Brother Tom, that everybody who dances is not a Christian?"

No, I don't mean that. I think a Christian might backslide and get so far away from God he might go to a dance, but he will be the most miserable person on the floor if he is a Christian; and if he enjoys it, he is not a Christian, for God's Holy Book says, "**Whosoever is born of God doth not commit** (continually) **sin; for His seed remaineth in him: and he cannot sin** (continually) **because he is born of God**" (I John 3:9). If you enjoy sin, you are not saved. You may sin, but no Christian is going to enjoy it. If you can sin and enjoy it, I wouldn't give you a nickel for your chance of ever getting to heaven. Christians, born-again people, do not enjoy sin.

"Well," this young lady said, "I'll never be one."

I said, "You never will; you'll never be saved until you are willing."

That was a three-week meeting. Toward the close of the meeting, I saw her come again. No one led her by the hand this time. She came bowed with conviction and fell at the altar and said, "I want to be saved, and whatever I have to turn away from, Brother Tom, I am willing turn loose from it."

She later married a friend of mine, as fine a Christian man as ever walked on two feet, and they have a lovely Christian home today. They have fine children and are happy in the Lord, but she would have gone to hell for sure if she had continued to say, "I will not give it up." She might have been in hell today, who knows? People turn their backs on Jesus because they are not willing to give up some things. That is one reason why it is so important today that Christians be separated from the world. It also makes it most important that our preaching give emphasis to the depravity of the human heart and point to the natural cravings of lost people for the pleasure of sin which lasts but a season. **"Will ye also go away?"**

V. THEY WENT AWAY BECAUSE OF PROCRASTINATION

People turn their backs on Jesus because they procrastinate; they put it off until another day. You know we often mention the fact that down in Mexico there are two words which they often say. One is "*Manana*" (tomorrow). The other is "*siesta* ." They sleep today and put off much that ought to be done until tomorrow. Do you know of any more backward country in the world? Think of all they have lost; think of all they might have had; think of all they might have gained if they had not said for centuries, "Wait until tomorrow."

Let me tell you, dear friends, I know of no instrument in the hands of the Devil that has sent more people to hell and caused more to turn their backs on the Son of God than those words, "Not now, Preacher, some other day."

I so often think when I stand up to preach in my auditorium of a man who sat back there under the balcony one week before Easter Sunday on Palm Sunday about four years ago. He was a 26 year old man who lifted his hand for prayer during the invitation, and by his uplifted hand indicated that he was a lost sinner and wanted me to pray for him. We prayed. As I remember, someone went to him and spoke to him. Others came that day but he did not. Before the next Sunday had come, he was burned to death in an awful automobile and truck accident out on Dixie Highway. I preached his funeral, and they shipped his body to be buried in the family graveyard down in the southern hills. His soul is in hell right now.

On Easter Sunday when the invitation was given, there came young man down the center aisle who is now preaching the gospel. He grabbed me by the hand and said, "Mr. Malone, you mentioned today a 26 year old man who sat in this church last Sunday whose funeral you have already preached. God being my helper, that is never going to happen to me. Tell me how to be saved."

Two young men — one is in the pulpit right now and the other is in hell. If a sinner says, "Tomorrow," and keeps saying it, he will go as straight to hell as any sinner ever went. If a Christian keeps putting off the matter of witnessing to his friends and family, he may never win them. One by one they pass to their Christless guilt and gloom. Write a letter today; make a phone call. Get your loved ones in for the night cometh when no man can work. "**Will ye also go away?**"

I wish I had time to preach another sermon on the next question, "**To whom shall we go?**" "**To whom shall we go?**" Did you ever think of it?"

Shall we go to the modernists? No. They don't know how to tell you to meet the hunger of the human heart.

Shall we turn to the world? No. When a sinner is dying and turns his face to the wall and looks right in the face of an open grave and an endless eternity, the world has nothing to offer him.

Shall we go to wisdom? No. We shall go to the One Who is the Fountain of all wisdom.

Shall we go to wealth? No. We'll go to the One Who owns the world and all that is in it
— the Son of God.

"**Will ye also go away?**" "**To whom shall we go, thou hast the words of eternal life?**"

CHAPTER EIGHT EVANGELISM AND SOUL-WINNING A DAILY BUSINESS

TEXT: "**And daily in the temple, and in every house they ceased not to teach and preach Jesus Christ**" (Acts 5:42).

Christianity is a daily business, a seven day a week job with no time off. The greatest tragedy of modern-day, twentieth century Christianity is that it has degenerated into a matter of Sunday church attendance rather than a daily living for Jesus. Jesus said, "**If any man will come after me, let him deny himself, and take up his cross daily, and follow me**" (Luke 9:23). When one reads the book of Acts, he is convinced that soul winning or personal evangelism was the main business of the early church and not just a matter of secondary importance.

A study of the word "**daily**" as it is used in the books of Acts is most stimulating and heart searching. The early church in Jerusalem, which won souls, overcame opposition, defied kings and kingdoms, brought fear and conviction to the hearts of multiplied thousands and made Jesus known everywhere, was a church with a daily ministry. They had a daily fellowship, for "**they continuing daily with one accord in the temple, and breaking bread from house to house, did eat their meat with gladness, and singleness of heart**" (Acts 2:46). The church grew daily, not just when revivals were held or during special seasons but daily for the record says "**the Lord added to the church daily such as should be saved**" (Acts 2:47).

Notice how that early church grew with no radio, no television no buildings, no newspapers, no Sunday School literature, no busses or cars, and no committees but with a Spirit-empowered program. Three thousand were saved in one service, and that number grew until immediately there were five thousand men alone. That group grew so rapidly that it was referred to as "**the multitude of them that believed**" (Acts 4:32). There were miracles wrought, prayer meetings held, persecutions endured and lying church members slain by the Holy Spirit, and the next account of the growth of the early church is given in Acts 5:14 where we read, **"And believers were the more added to the Lord, multitudes of both men and women**," no longer a multitude but multitudes.

This apostolic church accepted the challenge of the daily needs of lost humanity, for Peter and John on their way into the temple to pray saw a **"certain man lame from his mother's womb . . . whom they laid daily at the gate of the temple which is called beautiful**"(Acts 3:2).

Where did we ever get the idea that people need the Word of God on the Lord's Day only and that people can get saved on the Lord's Day only? Souls are perishing daily. We must be challenged by the daily needs of a lost and perishing people. The early church also carried on the "**daily ministrations**" (Acts 6:1) of material necessities for the saints of God which necessitated the appointment and election of seven Spirit-filled deacons.

As a result of this daily demonstration of Christianity, we begin to read of "**churches**" plural instead of the "**church**" singular. These early Christians went everywhere preaching the gospel. They launched an all-out campaign to evangelize the known world in their generation, and as a result, "**the churches were established in the faith and increased in number daily**" (Acts 16:5). The church today doing God's work in God's way and with God's power and by God's scriptural methods should produce other churches in needy communities.

These early Christians "**searched the Scriptures daily, whether those things were so**" (Acts 17:11) and daily went out to publish abroad what they found. Paul "**disputed . . . in the market daily with those that met with him**" (Acts 17:17) in the city of Athens and "**disputed daily in the school of one Tyrannus**" (Acts 19:9) in idolatrous Ephesus.

Now you say to me, "How did that church grow with such miraculous rapidity?"

I believe that the answer to that question lies in one thrilling and challenging verse. That verse ought to be the theme song and battle cry of every individual believer and every fundamental Bible-believing church throughout the world. That verse sums up in nineteen words the miracle of the early church; it was the "dynamic" of that successful group of believers. It describes their mode of operation.

That verse is Acts 5:42, **"And daily in the temple and from house to house they ceased not to teach and preach Jesus Christ."** This verse put in practice by any group of sincere Christians, large or small, in any community, city, or rural area will win souls, bring revivals, get results, cause miracles to unfold and produce a strong, powerful, and militant church "fair as the moon, clear as the sun, and terrible as an army with banners." One such center of scriptural church evangelism will bring a revival to our nation that will honor God, vindicate His Word, win the lost by the multitudes and put the armies of modernism to flight. Let us carefully and prayerfully examine the program of evangelism of this early church.

I. LET US SEE THEIR PERSISTANCE "DAILY"

These Christians were persistent. They were not sporadic or spasmodic. They were "**instant in season and out of season**" in their soul-winning and witnessing. It was not just a Sunday business with them but a daily business. Any church which expects to grow and reach multitude of men and women and children for Christ must have a daily ministry of evangelism. The church must have a daily calling and visitation program. Unsaved people must be visited not once, not twice, but dozens of times if need be to reach them for Christ. We must compel them to come in out of the highways and hedges that the house of the Lord may be filled.

On one occasion when one of the men of my church and I were visiting in a home, we had the wonderful joy to sit down around the kitchen table and lead the mother of six children to Christ. As we were leaving the home, I asked the man who was with me, "How many visits do you suppose the people of our church have made in that home?"

He replied, "I don't know but I will try to find out."

You see there was a child or two in that home which should have been in the Junior Department of our Sunday School and one or two in the Intermediate Department and one or two in other departments, and workers from all these departments had been visiting in that home for several weeks. In a day or two this man came to me and said, "Brother Tom, I have checked with the superintendents of these various departments, and I have found that approximately forty visits have been made in that home by the various workers of our church." Now you think of it; thirty-eight visits did not win a soul; thirty-nine visits did not do the job; but forty different visits won a precious soul to Jesus Christ! It takes persistence, sticking to the job, never giving up, and going day and night to win souls to Christ.

Some time ago when a group of our workers had gone out visitation work and were testifying in an after meeting as to the blessing of God upon their ministry, one lady said, "I have something to tell the group." She told this story.

"Tonight we went into a house where various workers of our church have been visiting for a year or so. I have been in the home number of times myself. When we went into the home tonight, the man of the house was trying to look at his favorite television program. When he saw who we were and realized we were from the Emmanuel Baptist Church, he said, 'Now listen, ladies. I have had my favorite television program interrupted every Monday night for more than a year. I get so nervous every Monday night that I can't enjoy myself. I have been sitting here shaking like a leaf and wondering when you would come to the door. I promise you,' he said, 'if you just let up on me a little and let me have one Monday night without being disturbed, I'll be in church next Sunday and have all the family with me.'"

We must not be afraid to bother people. Our business is too important. It cannot wait. The souls of men are at stake. God help us to be persistent.

II. LET US SEE THE PARTICIPANTS

This was not just the work of a group of preachers. These early Christians did not say, "Let the beloved pastor visit all the sick, win all the lost, and do all the work. Is that not what we hired him to do?" Every born-again person is to help in the winning of the lost. The deacons of the early church, men like Stephen and Philip, were soulwinners. Pastors who do not charge their people with their solemn obligation to win souls and then teach them how to do the job, grieve the Holy Spirit, fail to reach multitudes, and violate the plain teaching of God's Holy Word.

Let us see this truth in Ephesians 4:11-12.

"And he gave some, apostles; and some, prophets; and some evangelists; and some pastors and teachers; for the perfecting (or equipping) **of the saints for the work of the ministry, for the edifying of the body of Christ."**

Every choir member, every board member, every Sunday School teacher, every church member should be taught to go out after souls and bring them into the house of God to hear the Word and be saved. The tragedy of our weak, anemic Christianity of these days is that many preachers, missionaries, and evangelists do not win souls. A Christian who will not win souls is an enigma! He is like a barber who refuses to cut hair and a clerk who refuses to sell goods and a salesman who never sells anything.

III. LET US SEE THE PARTNERSHIP "TWO BY TWO"

We believe these Christians went out **"two by two**." Jesus called two brethren to leave their fishing nets and follow Him. John sent two of his disciples to question Jesus, and Jesus sent out the seventy **"two by two"** and taught that in the mouth of two or three witnesses a truth would be established.

Notice these Scriptures,

- **"And he called unto Him the twelve and began to send them forth two and two"** (Mark 6:7);
- **"He sendeth forth two of his disciples"** (Mark 11:1);
- **"And after these things the Lord appointed other seventy also, and sent them two and two before His face into every city and**

place, whither he himself would come" (Luke 10:1).

There were two heavenly messengers at the empty tomb on the morning of the resurrection of Jesus, and two men in white apparel were sent down from heaven when He ascended from the Mt. of Olives to go back into the presence of His Father. In Ecclesiastes 4:9 we read that **"Two are better than one; because they have a good reward for their labor."**

Yes, we believe that God's divinely appointed way to win the lost is for the church to go out two by two daily to witness for Christ. In the church where I have now served as pastor for almost sixteen years, we see large groups of people saved every Sunday. It matters not who is preaching; it matters not whether the sermon is a good one or a poor one, souls are saved just the same. People have been going out two by two during the week to win them to Christ, and they walk forward with them on Sunday mornings and Sunday evenings as they come to make a public profession of their faith in the Lord Jesus Christ. I have known one man and his wife to have as high as fourteen grown men and women come to be saved in one single service.
Jesus was never too busy to win souls, and He was a personal worker. If we are too busy to go out two by two to win the lost, then we are busier than God ever intended us to be.

IV. LET US SEE THE PLAN — "FROM HOUSE TO HOUSE"

These early Christians went from house to house. They did not wait for the world to come to the church.

They went to the lost and won them from house to house and brought them to be baptized and take fellowship with the local church. Sometimes preachers fail to go from house to house, claiming to be too busy in their studies and offices. Paul was not too busy or too unconcerned to go from house to house. He testified to the Ephesian elders that he had "**served the Lord with all humility of mind and with many tears**" . . . and had "**kept back nothing that was profitable unto you, and have taught you publicly, and from house to house**" (Acts 20:19-20). The "**house to house**" ministry is just as important and perhaps more so than the public ministry. In fact, the lack of results in much of the pulpit ministry can be charged to lack of effort and tears in the **"house to house"** ministry.

The other day I read a fine article in a Christian periodical on "How often should I visit?" The article was written around a recent survey that was made by the National Retail Dry Goods Association It revealed some figures that throw a lot of light on this problem. Many teachers and workers wonder how often they should call on prospects and absentees. Perhaps this report might help you:

48% of the salesmen make one call and quit.
25% of the salesmen make two calls and quit.
88% of the salesmen quit after one, two, or three calls. 12% of the salesmen keep on calling.

The 12% who keep on call do 80% of the business.
The 88% who quit by the third call do only 20% of the business

Are you included in the 12% or the 88%? We are to go from house to house to visit the sick, the lost, the bereaved and the delinquent. This is God's way, the Bible way, the only way.

V. LET US SEE THE PLACE — "IN THE TEMPLE"

The evangelism of the early church in the book of Acts was church-centered evangelism. It was an evangelism which had as its base of operation the local church. I am for any type of evangelism which is not unscriptural, whether it be union or cooperative evangelism, child evangelism, or missionary evangelism. The Scriptures teach that churches in the New Testament days were great centers of evangelism. Pastors are wrong who say, "My job is to teach the saints, and I will leave the winning of the lost to the evangelist." Paul told Timothy to **"Do the work of an evangelist."**

He also complimented the church at Thessalonica saying, **"For from you sounded out the word of the Lord not only in Macedonia and Achaia, but also in every place your faith to God-ward is spread abroad; so that we need not to speak anything"** (I Thessalonians 1:8).

Scriptural church evangelism is important because people not only need to be saved but they need to be baptized and unite with a fundamental, Bible-believing, soul-winning church. They need to be taught the Word of God, the great Christian doctrines, the importance of tithing and soul-winning; and this is the responsibility of every local church.

VI. LET US SEE THE PREACHING — "THEY CEASED NOT TO PREACH AND

TEACH JESUS CHRIST"

The apostolic, evangelistic, soul-winning church of Jerusalem did not preach a program but they preached a Person!

- They did not deal in abstract theories and philosophies, but they lifted up and magnified a real and living Saviour.
- They did not deal with technicalities while their generation rushed on to hell, they majored on the message of life as is found in the Son of God.
- They did not preach to please everybody and offend nobody, they preached with the power and demonstration of the Holy Spirit and brought conviction and fear to the heart of the ungodly.

They lifted up Jesus and magnified Him in all His glorious attributes.

You no doubt have heard the simple yet wonderful story of the young, highly-trained pastor who went to his new appointment intent on impressing his flock with his education. After a few sermons delivered from the head and not from the heart, after the sheep had come a few times to feed and found nothing to eat but chaff, he found a note on his pulpit. The note contained these words, "**Sir, we would see Jesus**." It angered him at first but later convicted him and brought him to his knees to cry out in prayer, "Oh, Father, help me so to preach that the people will see Jesus."

Recently one of our young preachers in the Seminary met me and said, "Brother Tom, pray for my church. I want to see people saved, and the hunger of my heart is to make Jesus known to them."

He was so moved with emotion he could hardly speak; his lips trembled and his eyes swam with tears of love and tender compassion. I promised to pray, and as I walked on my way the thought came to me, "He won't have to wait long to see people saved. When Jesus is preached from a broken heart, when sermons are bathed in tears and saturated with prayer and backed up by a holy life, men and women are going to come to God."

The following Monday morning I met the same young preacher, and I saw a strange light in his face! "Brother Tom, yesterday nine people were saved in my church!"

You can be a soul winner; you, too, can win the lost. God give us the compassion, the power of the Holy Spirit, and faith to do God's work by God's prescribed methods.

CHAPTER NINE WHAT IS CLOSEST TO THE HEART OF JESUS?

TEXT: "**And that repentance and remission of sins should be preached in His name among all nations beginning at Jerusalem**" (Luke 24:47).

If you and I could sit down and talk for ten minutes, when the ten minutes were over, what would be my opinion as to what was closest to your heart? When the ten minutes were over and you went away, I wonder what you would say is closest to the heart of Brother Tom? Jesus left no doubt about what was closest to His heart.

I'm going to speak to you this morning from five different Scriptures I'm reading one of them at this time, and we might call it our text.

"**And as they thus spake, Jesus himself stood in the midst of them, and saith unto them,**

Peace be unto you. But they were terrified and affrighted, and supposed that they had seen a spirit. And he said unto them, Why are ye troubled? and why do thoughts arise in your hearts? Behold my hands and my feet, that it is I myself: handle me, and see; for a spirit hath not flesh and bones, as ye see me have. And when he had thus spoken, he shewed them his hands and his feet. And while they yet believed not for joy, and wondered, he said unto them, Have ye here any meat? And they gave him a piece of a broiled fish, and of an honeycomb. And he took it, and did eat before them. And he said unto them, These are the words which I spake unto you, while I was yet with you, that all things must be fulfilled, which were written in the law of Moses, and in the prophets, and in the psalms, concerning me. Then opened he their understanding, that they might understand the scriptures, And said unto them, Thus it is written, and thus it behoved Christ to suffer, and to rise from the dead the third day: And that repentance and remission of sins should be preached in his name among all nations, beginning at Jerusalem. And ye are witnesses

of these things. And, behold, I send the promise of my Father upon you: but tarry ye in the city of Jerusalem, until ye be endued with power from on high. And he led them out as far as to Bethany, and he lifted up his hands, and blessed them. And it came to pass, while he blessed them, he was parted from them, and carried up into heaven. And they worshipped him, and returned to Jerusalem with great joy: And were continually in the temple, praising and blessing God. Amen**" (Luke 24:36-53).

For our text notice verse 47: **"That repentance and remission of sins should be preached in His name among all nations, beginning at Jerusalem."**

Five times in the first five books of the New Testament we have recorded by four different writers what is called the GREAT COMMISSION.

Jesus Christ has given a commission to the church. If you want to know what is closest to the heart of the Lord Jesus Christ, notice the five times that the Great Commission is given in the first five book of the New Testament. Of course, you know the answer. The thing closest to the heart of Jesus Christ was the matter of soul-winning—seeing people saved, seeing people hear about Jesus, Who could satisfy the longing of the heart, forgive sin, and save people from sin. Every time you find Jesus in the Bible He is interested in somebody's soul. He was the greatest personal worker the world has ever known. The greatest sermons and discourses He ever gave were not given to great multitudes of people, but, in many instances, they were given to one person.

You see Him sitting at Jacob's Well in John 4. He is thirsty and tired, but there is a longing in His heart that supersedes His desire for water and His desire for rest. A woman comes who is lost. Jesus talks with her and leads her to a saving knowledge of Himself. The disciple come later with food to eat. He says, **"I have meat to eat that ye know not of"** (John 4:32).

You see Him one night in the city of Jerusalem, and perhaps He and His anxious inquirer were standing out in the beautiful Judean moonlight. From His blessed lips that night there came the most vital and important message that ever fell on human ears, the message of the new birth.

That message was not given in the temple to a great congregation of people, it was not spoken to thronging multitudes on the hillsides. It was spoken to one man—a lost, rich, religious ruler.

Jesus was not too busy to talk alone with one man or woman. The preacher who is too busy to speak with one lost man or woman will probably never build a large church or speak to great congregations.

I think I am safe in saying that the thing that was closest to the heart of Jesus Christ was to see people saved. The thing that was on His heart all the time, the thing for which He came into the world He expressed in Luke 19:10 in these words, "**The Son of Man is come to seek and to save that which is lost**."

In Matthew, Mark, Luke, John and Acts Jesus gives the commission to the church.

Every church, every church member, every Christian and every preacher ought to be interested in knowing what the commission to the church is. What did the Lord Jesus Christ, before He left this world, tell the church that the church's job is? What is our greatest responsibility? What is the thing that five times Jesus talked about just before the heavens burst with the glory of God and He was received out of sight? What is the thing that five times Jesus mentioned and indicated that it meant more to Him than anything else taught in the Word of God?

I. THE PROMISE OF HIS PRESENCE (MATTHEW 28:20)

In the closing verses of the Gospel of Matthew for the first time in the New Testament, we find the commission of the Lord Jesus Christ to the church. There we read, "**All power is given unto me in heaven and in earth. Go ye therefore, and teach all nations, baptizing them in the name of the Father, and of the Son and of the Holy Ghost: Teaching them to observe all things whatsoever I have**

commanded you: and lo, I am with you alway, even unto the end of the world" (Matthew 28:18-20).

The amazing and wonderful thing about the five times Jesus commissions the church to win souls is that He makes a separate and distinct promise to the church or to the Christian who will win lost souls. He says, "***If you carry out My commission, you can depend on My presence.***"

Every one of these five times He guarantees the Christian something. Every one of these five times He assures the Christian of something different if the Christian would be a soul winner. Here He says, "***If you go into all the world, if you make the gospel known if you put soul-winning first in your church, in your heart, in your life, in your time, if you put soulwinning at the top of the list***, "LO, I AM WITH YOU ALWAY, EVEN UNTO THE END OF THE AGE."

There is a sense in which He is with every Christian. There is a sense in which God is with a Christian if he never lifts his hand to win a soul. There is a sense in which God is with me if I never speak to another lost soul from now until my dying day. He came into my heart years ago. He will never leave me nor forsake me. God Almighty is with me all the time, anywhere and everywhere.

But here's something special: Jesus said, "***If you go into all the world*** . . ." Your world starts right where you are. It starts in your family. It starts on your street. It starts in your office. It starts wherever you touch one single human life.

Jesus said, "***If you go to people with the gospel, lo, I am with you alway, even unto the end of the age.***"

I think of some of the wonderful moments of my fellowship with the Lord Jesus Christ, and I've enjoyed some wonderful moments, thank God. I think about times when I go yonder into my office, close the door and get down on my knees with God's Book open before my face and ask God to speak to me and then tell God what I have on my heart. Those are wonderful moments.

Every night before bedtime, I take the Word of God and gather my family about me and read a chapter of God's Holy Word and we bow our heads and thank God for His goodness upon our home and upon our family. Those are wonderful moments. God is with us when we pray as a family.

But the one time in all the Word of God that the Lord Jesus Christ promised His presence in a special way to a Christian is when that Christian is in the act of soul-winning. "*If you go*," He said, "**lo, I am with you alway, even unto the end of the age**."

It is a mystery to me why it is so hard to get people to do what Jesus taught they are supposed to do; that is, to witness to the lost. Never am I more conscious of His presence than when I am out to win a soul to Him. I am thinking of a Sunday afternoon some time ago when my daughter and I went out on a Sunday afternoon to go from house to house to find the lost and unchurched. I could preach a whole sermon on miraculous things which have happened on one street while doing such work. On this particular occasion as I knocked at the door of one home, a middle-aged lady came to the door. She was in tears, and it was evident that she was in great distress. I said to her, "I am Tom Malone, and my daughter and I are out inviting people to come to the service tonight at the Emmanuel Baptist Church."

"Oh Brother Tom," she said, "I have heard you many times on the radio. I am so glad you came. I am in deep distress; please come in quickly." She continued, "My son is back here in the kitchen; he is a war veteran. While he was in the service, his wife proved unfaithful to him and has now left him. He has a knife in his hand and is about to take his life. Won't you please help him?"

I went back into the kitchen and standing over by the sink was a fine looking young man, shaking like a leaf in the wind and weeping like a child. I took him by the hand and led him to chair and told him of One Who could forgive him of all his sin and Who would be a friend and companion and would never prove unfaithful to him. I had the joy of leading both mother and son to a saving knowledge of Jesus Christ. God knew where that boy was and knew he was close to an eternal hell. He led me there; He gave me words to say. He was with me. **"And lo, I am with you alway, even unto the end of the world."**

You may never have the backing and approval of great religious machines and denominational programs, but you can reckon upon the presence of God if you really want to be a soul winner.

II. THE PROMISE OF HIS PROTECTION (MARK 16:15-18)

"And he said unto them, Go ye into all the world, and preach the gospel to every creature.

He that believeth and is baptized shall be saved; but he that believeth not shall be dammed. And these signs shall follow them that believe; In my name shall they cast out devils; they shall speak with new tongues; They shall take up serpents; and if they drink any deadly thing, it shall not hurt them; they shall lay hands on the sick, and they shall recover" (Mark 16:15-18).

Here in the Book of Mark where Jesus gives the Great Commission, He gives it with the promise of His protection. Notice the five things that Jesus promises that His disciples were to have victory over:

- They could cast out devils.
- They could speak with new tongues, or new languages.
- They could take up serpents.
- If they drank any deadly thing, it would not hurt them.
- They were to have victory over disease.

I have often given thought and prayer to this passage of Scripture in Mark 16 because, beyond any shadow of doubt, there are some difficulties attached to it. We make no claim to scholarship; we are merely a student of the Scriptures, but there are two or three things we believe to be true concerning this passage which ought to be mentioned here.

First, from verse 9 in this chapter to the end, through verse there is a question about the inspiration of it. Scofield footnotes make plain that these verses are not found in the two oldest and most authoritative manuscripts, the Sinaitic and Vaticanus. Nevertheless, it was quoted as we have it by the early church saints and soon after Pentecost, and in all probability it is a part of the sacred writings, inspired of God.

A second matter that should be mentioned is that this particular Scripture might be said to be apostolic in nature. The signs Jesus gave here, which were to follow preaching the gospel and winning the lost, were definitely apostolic. The apostles had these signs in their ministry. For instance, Paul, on the island of Malta, was bitten by a venomous serpent, which did him no harm because God was with him to protect him. His work was not done, and until his work of soul-winning was finished, God would allow no harm to come to him.

The third thing, and to me the most wonderful, is that beyond any shadow of doubt the passage is designed to teach that God's special protection is promised to the soul winner and the angels of the Lord encamp around about those who seek to do His will and send His Word to the ends of the earth. I have the assurance in my heart that no evil could possibly befall me as I seek to win the lost except it come from the hand of God as a part of His directive will for my life and ministry.

I know that many of God's chosen saints have laid down their lives for the gospel's sake, have been torn asunder, thrown to the wild beasts and burned at the stake, but I believe that by the cruel persecution and death of these saints of God they have won more people and sent the gospel further into the regions of the world than they ever could have by living.

I have sometimes felt it was almost unnecessary to speak concerning the protective power of God for soul winners.

So few of God's people today are out in the hot part of the battle; so few are willing to endanger themselves and hazard their life for the cause of Christ. So many today play it absolutely safe, take no risk whatever and keep a safe distance away from the possibility of embarrassment and persecution. The same God who sent earthquakes to tear down prisons and sent angels to jail to liberate His messenger will protect the child of God who dares to walk with

Him in this all important matter of soul-winning.

God protects his soul winners. Thank God for this. If you will consecrate your services this day to the Lord, put soul-winning first in your life, now and forever, God's hand will be on your life in a most wonderful and in a special way. I have been in places as a preacher from which I do not believe I could have come out unscathed and unharmed had it not been for His assisting grace and His overcoming power.

III. THE PROMISE OF HIS PROGRAM (LUKE 24:46-47)

In the Book of Luke, Jesus outlines His program in the Great Commission. He says, **"Thus it is written, and thus it behooved Christ to suffer, and to rise from the dead the third day; And that repentance and remission of sins should be preached in his name among all nations**

(Now watch; I want to dwell on this!) **beginning at Jerusalem"** (Luke 24:46-47).

Jesus said, "*The gospel must go to the ends of the earth.*" Where is this church to start? Where were the twelve disciples to begin? Where is this Pentecostal church, which is filled with the Holy Spirit of God, to start? Where are you to start? Jesus said, "***It's going to all nations but beginning at Jerusalem.***"

Why? It was at Jerusalem that wicked people crucified the Son of God, and they were as lost as the heathen in the darkest part of the world. Jesus is teaching here that before you can send the gospel to Africa and India, you must evangelize at home. That is the program for the church and for any New Testament Christian church. Start at home. The biggest farce in the world is to send a dollar to Africa and not knock on a door in Pontiac or some other city. It's hypocrisy and it's mockery!

Word came to me some time ago of a missionary circle in which some members (not all of them, thank God) said "Visitation business is not our business. We're a missionary circle."

Yes, it is your business. The missionary program for the church I pastor starts in the city of Pontiac. If we can't have a missionary circle that believes that, we won't have one.

First at Jerusalem!

Do you know why some people don't win souls at home? They've never seen the truth that Jesus taught, the truth to start at Jerusalem. Do you know what it means? It means to start at yourself. Be sure you know Christ as your personal Saviour. Start winning souls at Jerusalem.

The program of the fundamental church of this age is to make Christ known by radio, by preaching, by paper, by house to house visitation, by word of mouth—every way we possibly can. That was the program of the early church. That was the program of the church at Pentecost. That was the program of the church filled with the Holy Ghost. That was the program of the early church. " **Daily in the temple, and in every house, they ceased not to teach and preach Jesus Christ**" (Acts 5:42).

Let me tell you, there is many a church member and many a man or woman who criticizes the soul-winning program, criticizes the preacher that preaches it, when the only thing that person needs is an old-fashioned dose of salvation, repentance of sin and getting right with God.

The program of Jesus is soul-winning, and if we don't put that first, we can't do anything right for God.

The biggest mockery in the world is to have a Christian School or a church that doesn't win souls! The biggest mockery on earth is to have a seminary in a church, as we have, if we are not winning people to Christ. A missionary circle which does not win souls at home is a religious farce!

I expect every board member of our church to have a part in soul winning, and I wouldn't give five cents for any member of any board that wouldn't help win souls to Jesus Christ. They're not worthy of the name. They ought to get off the board. They're not interested in the souls of men and women.

I wouldn't give you a nickel for a Sunday school teacher who had no interest in knocking on doors and telling people about Jesus and trying to get people saved. I wouldn't give you a nickel for a choir member that sings, "O, How I Love Jesus," and fights a program that Jesus instituted.

It's hypocritical, a farce, wicked, and a positive indication of backsliding in the heart of anybody that's not interested in it. If I weren't interested in it, I just wouldn't tell anybody for anything in the world, because it surely makes it look mighty bad for you. It's closest to the heart of Jesus.

Isn't it strange that what was closest to the heart of Jesus is furthest from the heart of the average Christian? Do you understand it?

Do you understand how it could be that the thing closest to Jesus' heart is so often furthest from the hearts of so-called professing people of God? I wonder sometimes if the reason for it is that the person has not started at Jerusalem? That is starting at home, starting with getting saved yourself. I believe every really saved person is interested in putting forth some effort to see people saved.

I heard some years ago of a young woman who had graduated from a Christian school and applied as a missionary candidate to a board then working in China. She was from a California city where there was a rather large population of Chinese people. A member of the examining board said, "Have you ever won a Chinese to Christ?"

"Oh no," she said, "I haven't been to China yet. I'll win them after I get there."

The member of the missionary board said, "If you don't love the Chinese enough here in America to win them to Jesus, you will have no success at winning them after you get to China. I am going to vote against accepting you. I don't believe you will ever make a good missionary."

I agree with him. If you don't love the souls of men enough to win them right here and right now, you never will win them. "**Beginning at Jerusalem**"—there is only one starting place and that is right where you are now.

IV. THE PROMISE OF His PEACE (JOHN 20:19-23)

The fourth time the Great Commission is given is in John. Here Jesus guaranteed something else to the soul winner.

"**Then the same day at evening, being the first day of the week, when the doors were shut where the disciples were assembled for fear of the Jews, came Jesus and stood in the midst, and saith unto them, Peace be unto you. And when He had so said, he shewed unto them his hands and his side. Then were the disciples glad, when they saw the Lord. Then said Jesus to them again, Peace be unto you: as my Father hath sent me, even so I send you**" (John 20:19-21).

Jesus said, "*As you go discharging that commission, giving that gospel, you are going to have great peace in your life.*"

We talk about twisted personalities. The only thing wrong with some people's personalities is that they are not doing the will of God. The greatest adjustment in human life is to be in God's will and to be doing what God wants you to. That will adjust more personalities than anything else in the world. That will do more for human life than anything else on this earth. The greatest peace that ever came into the heart of a human being is the peace of knowing he has done his best as a Christian to see people saved.

Some of my church people sent me a message a few days ago to go see a man in the hospital. I went to see that man three times. The first time I went to see him, I could get nowhere. But I knew the man was lost and sick; so I went back the second time and stood by his bed. He did not want to hear what I had to say, but God Almighty had given me the responsibility to witness to the lost. I stood at that bedside and read John 3:16 and Acts 16:31 and other verses showing how to be saved. I said, "O God, when I turn from this bed in a moment and walk out of this hospital, I want to be able to say that that man on his dying bed heard the gospel of Jesus Christ. Father, when some day I stand up yonder before Your throne, I don't want the blood of that man's soul to be on my hands."

He did not get saved. Later I got a message, "He's worse now." I went back the third time. I said, "Friend, can you hear me?"

"Yes."

"Can you understand what I am saying?" "Yes."

I went over it again. I bowed my head and prayed. I believe his eyes were wide open during the prayer. I don't think he ever showed any interest.

The following day the message came that he was dead. His destiny was forever sealed. There was no more chance. Never would he hear the gospel again.

When the message came, I said to my wife, "Thank God I did my best."

Listen, friend, death and disaster strike everywhere. It's happening to your neighbors, your friends, your loved ones. Members of this audience today have people who are on their way to hell and who are near to you.

How will it be when the doctor says, "Your daddy is dying," or, "Your sister is dead." Can you lift your voice toward heaven and say, "God, I did my best; I put You first in my life, my heart, my home, my business, and I tried to make Jesus known to some lost soul."

There is a great peace in my heart today because I did my best to win him. His blood will not be on my hands in the day of reckoning. **"Peace be unto you, as my father hath sent me even so send I you."**

V. THE PROMISE OF HIS POWER (ACTS 1:8)

The Great Commission is given the fifth time in Acts 1:8, "**But ye shall receive power, after that the Holy Ghost is come upon you; and ye shall be witnesses unto me in Jerusalem, and in all Judea, and in Samaria, and unto the uttermost part of the earth**."

You say, "Brother Tom, I want to but I can't. I'm not strong enough."

Listen, friend, neither am I. There's not a man or woman in this building any weaker than I am. But let me tell you, Jesus guarantees His power. He said that you have the power of the Holy Spirit to win souls to Jesus Christ. I'm here to say today that every man, every woman, every Christian who wants to see people saved and wants to evangelize this city and send the gospel to the ends of the earth can have that power of God to do it if he wants it. But it will cost something to have that power.

- You cannot have the world and have that power also.
- You cannot love and harbor sin in your heart and have that power also.
- You cannot be filled with your own plans, your own ambitions, and your own desires and be filled with that power.

God fills clean vessels and empty vessels.

How about it, friend? Are you saved? Are you interested in making the gospel known? That is what is closest to the heart of Jesus. That is what I have on my heart. That is the commission to the church. That is marching orders. The Captain of the church says, "These are my orders."

God give us men and women who will salute and say, "Ask for me, dear Jesus. I'm ready, and I'll take Your gospel wherever You want it to go, and I'll be a humble, faithful witness for You." We have the promise of His presence, His protection, His program, His peace, and His power. What more do we need?

CHAPTER TEN HOW A CHURCH SHOULD PREPARE FOR A REVIVAL CAMPAIGN

TEXT: "**If my people, which are called by my name shall humble themselves, and pray, and seek my face, and turn from their wicked ways; then will I hear from heaven, and will forgive their sin, and will heal their land**" (II Chronicles 7:14).

We almost hesitate to give a lecture on this subject for fear that someone might think we are taking the assumptive step of a "know-it-all." However, God knows and we know in our own heart that this is not the case. We certainly do not know all the answers and all the details involved in a church's preparing for a revival campaign. Through the years from other men of God, from experience, and from making mistakes we have gathered a few helpful things which have proven to be a great blessing and have meant the salvation of many souls in revival campaigns here in the Emmanuel Baptist Church in Pontiac, Michigan, over a period of sixteen years.

During the years preachers have written us, many of them young preachers without experience, asking how a church should go about getting ready for the coming of an evangelist for a revival campaign. So as best we know how we would like to make suggestions to churches, which, if carried out, we believe will prove a great blessing to the church, a blessing and help to the evangelist, and most important of all will result in the salvation of many more precious souls.

It has been our experience, and I have found that it has been the experience of many God-called evangelists, that when they go to churches to conduct a revival campaign, the pastor and people expect the evangelist to bring the revival with him. No planning or preparation has been made before the revival campaign starts, and in many instances there has been very little prayer about the matter. Many times the only thing that is done is the announcement from the pulpit and the announcement in the church bulletin that an evangelist is coming and that a week or two weeks have been set apart for a series of special services.

I realize fully that only God can give a revival. Revival comes from God. However, the Bible plainly teaches that God's people have a responsibility and should make every effort in the world to discharge that responsibility and be prepared for a revival campaign.

God says, "**If my people, which are called by my name**," shall do four things:

- **Humble themselves**,
- **Turn from their wicked ways**,
- **Seek my face**,
- **Pray**,

" . . . **then will I hear from heaven, and will forgive their sins, and will heal their land**."

There is a human responsibility in having revivals in churches. Notice that the human responsibility must be discharged before the Divine blessings begin. Revivals do not just happen. Revivals are the result of scriptural planning, preparing and praying.

Nearly sixteen years ago when we bought the Castle Inn Building and started the work of the Emmanuel Baptist Church, there was a large steel safe or vault which was a part of the building. One day I sat down in front of the safe door and began to turn the dial to try to open the door, but though I used many combinations, the door remained fast closed. After a few minutes of this fruitless frustration, I stepped to the phone and called the real estate office from whom we had purchased the building and asked for the combination. I was given four numbers to which the dial must be turned. When this combination was used, the door opened immediately. Now God has given us a combination which if followed will always, without fail, unlock the windows of heaven and bring a flood tide of revival blessing. The trouble in so many instances is that pastors and churches will not use God's formula for revival as set forth in II Chronicles 7:14.

In the Emmanuel Baptist Church we have a deacon board composed of seven members. In the first place, these men are truly saved. They are born-again children of God. They study the Word of God. They are empowered by the Holy Spirit. They live separated lives. They do not drink nor smoke. They are quiet, honorable, godly men. They visit the sick and win the lost and teach the saints. That is the only kind of man who is fit to be on a deacon board or any other board in the church.

It has been our experience in recent revivals that having seven different committees, each headed by a deacon, has been very successful in helping the entire church to prepare for a revival campaign. These deacons head these seven committees, and they appoint as many people as they need to do the special work of that committee. A committee might have five or six on it or it might have thirty or forty, according to the need. This uses scores of people in the church for at least a month ahead of time in preparing and working for the campaign. This adds emphasis to the campaign in the hearts and minds of the people of the church. I will list these seven committees and how they are to operate.

I. PRAYER COMMITTEE

We know there can be no revival without prayer — earnest, concentrated prayer; long seasons of prayer; and regular prayer. A committee is organized to arrange for various kinds of prayer meetings.

1. First of all, cottage prayer meetings.

For a full month in advance people's names and addresses and the time of the prayer meeting are secured and announced from the pulpit. In these meetings the groups are usually not large, but neighbors meet together in a home and have an appointed time and place for prayer for the revival and for the salvation of the lost. Remember that Jesus said, **"that if two of you shall agree on earth as touching anything that they shall ask, it shall be done for them of my father which is in heaven"** (Matthew 18:19).

- Sunday School departments meet together in their council meetings for seasons of prayer.

- Church boards are asked to meet at least once, if not more, before the campaign starts for prayer. If the board members and leaders of the church do not lead the way in the matter of prayer, there will be very little revival.

- Special emphasis is given to prayer in the mid-week service.

- Sunday School classes, especially the adult and young people's classes, are asked to set aside a night during the week for at least one week before the revival starts to have a special season of prayer asking God's blessing upon the revival campaign.

- A special prayer meeting is held by the choir and all accompanists and singers.

II. PERSONAL WORK COMMITTEE

We believe that God uses personal work to win souls to Jesus Christ. I have had people say to me, "I do not like to see folks spoken to during the invitation and during the services because I believe that the Holy Spirit should do that work."

I do not agree with this in any sense of the word. The Holy Spirit must do the work, of course. We lean entirely upon Him, but the Spirit of God usually works through a human agency. If the Holy Spirit did all the work, there would be no need for an evangelist. There would be no need for a pastor. There would be no need for anyone to stand up and preach. All that we would have to do is just let the Spirit of God speak to people's hearts and show them what to do. We believe that God uses yielded, Spirit-filled people in personal work.

In John 16:7-11 we read: "**Nevertheless I tell you the truth; It is expedient for you that that I go away: for if I go not away, the Comforter will not come unto you; but if I depart, I will send him unto you. And when he is come, he will reprove the world of sin, and of righteousness, and of judgment: Of sin, because they** believe not on me; Of righteousness, because I go to my Father, and ye see me no more; Of judgment, because the prince of this world is judged."** Notice that Jesus said, **"I will send him unto you"** in verse 11. The Holy Spirit works through you.

Everyone interested in personal work should be called together in a special group for one or two meetings before the campaign starts.

They should be briefed on how to speak to people, how to lead them to Christ, and how to come forward with them in the meeting, stand with them never leaving them standing alone, go with them into the inquiry room, and how to take the Word of God and lead them to a saving knowledge of Jesus Christ. We believe that it is perfectly proper and of the Lord to have people stationed in various parts of the auditorium watching for the uplifted hands of unsaved people so they can be useful in helping and assisting those people to go forward.

After the campaign is over, the personal workers' committee is responsible to see that every convert; in fact, every person that comes forward, is followed up, dealt with in the home from the Word of God about assurance, baptism, church membership, and going on with the Lord. These new converts need to be taught how to get into the Sunday school, the necessity of attending prayer meeting, tithing their income, studying the Word of God, and all that has to do with living the Christian life. They need to be shown the importance of having a fundamental, Bible-believing, soul-winning local church as their church home.

III. PUBLICITY COMMITTEE

This is a most important committee. It has been our experience that no matter how well a church is known or how well-known the evangelist might be who is coming to conduct the revival meeting there should be publicity before the campaign starts.

- It has been our experience that having enough brochures or pieces of advertising printed to put into every home in the city, no matter how large or small the city might be, is a paying proposition. This advertising material should be of first-class quality. It takes some fifteen thousand pieces of literature to put one in each home in our city of approximately one hundred thousand people. This is always done at least one week before the revival campaign starts.

- Radio advertising should be used at every advantage. Spot paid announcements are effective plus regular radio programs.

- Newspaper advertising should be used not just the Saturday before the meeting starts but at least two or three Saturdays before the campaign gets under way.

IV. ENTERTAINMENT COMMITTEE

This we feel is also an important committee. It has to do with arranging for every detail of the entertainment of the evangelist or evangelistic party. First of all, the arrangements to see that he is met at the train or airport; arrangements for a room and accommodations for meals, and all that is involved in the entertainment of the evangelist or evangelistic party. This committee should arrange for the transportation to and from the meeting each night so that the pastor, who has many responsibilities and much on his heart and mind during a campaign, will not have to discharge this responsibility.

I might suggest that it has been our experience that it always works well for an evangelist to be placed either in a nice quiet motel or hotel rather than in a home. This is not because the evangelist is antisocial, or neither is it because he is too good to stay in a private home.

He needs quiet; he needs to be able to rest, to study and pray, and to take care of correspondence and other work that every preacher of the Gospel has all the time.

Usually when staying in a home, though it is a home of lovely, wonderful, gracious Christian people, the evangelist is obligated to do so much entertaining, to carry on a good deal of the conversation, and, therefore, is not at his best when the time comes for the revival service.

We feel it is not best to take the evangelist around to different homes for one or more meals every day. The average preacher does not care to eat this much, and usually it is not best for him physically and does not work out to the best advantage of the meeting.

The little expense involved in providing an evangelist a private room in a motel or hotel and his meals wherever he feels best to eat them certainly is well worth the cost to any church.

There might be visiting preachers who shall come to spend a night or more during the revival campaign. This committee could be responsible for their entertainment also.

V. SPECIAL NIGHTS COMMITTEE

We have found that it works well to plan a number of special nights during the course of a revival campaign. These special nights are numerous such as Church Night, Family Night, Youth Night, Neighbor Night, Ladies Night, Men's Night, Pack-A-Pew Night, Sunday School Night, etc.

1. Church Night.

On Church Night an all-out effort should be made to have every member of the church present. On that night church members should be asked to stand, and the percentage of the entire membership which are present should be announced.

2. Family Night.

This is the night when all the families are urged to have every member of their family relation-ship present. Usually some nice little award is given to the family with the largest number present.

3. Bring-A-Neighbor Night.

On "neighbor" night every Christian is urged to bring one person who has not previously attended the revival campaign. A committee usually arranges to pin a flower on the one who is brought and the one who brings them. This is done at the entrances to the auditorium as the people come in.

We have seen as many as two hundred new people brought in one night, many of whom would be unsaved when they come.

4. Pack-A-Pew Night.

Several days before the campaign starts, each row of seats in the building is assigned to a captain or leader. His responsibility is to have his or her row of seats completely filled on "Pack-A-Pew" night. By this method we have seen large auditoriums filled on week nights in campaigns.

5. Sunday School Night.

On Sunday School Night every superintendent and teacher and officer and pupil is urged to be present. Departments are recognized separately from the Nursery through the Adult Department. This must be well planned in advance by announcements in each department and class. A card advertising this night should be placed in the mail to everyone on the Sunday school rolls.

6. Father and Son, Mother and Daughter Night.

All fathers are asked to bring a son and all mothers to bring a daughter. People without children can "adopt" a boy or girl for this night. Many neighborhood children are reached on this night who may not attend any church or who perhaps attend a church where the gospel is not preached.

These six special nights can be used on the week nights and repeated if necessary during the second week of the campaign. Other special nights which sometimes prove effective are Ladies' Night, Men's Night, and Youth Night.

VI. SPECIAL DELEGATIONS COMMITTEE

We find that churches enjoy cooperating together to a certain extent even in local church revivals; that is, the preacher and people of other churches usually are very gracious about coming on certain nights and may be bringing special music. The preacher and his delegation is acknowledged. This helps the attendance of the meeting. It gives the pastor of the visiting delegation an opportunity to hear the evangelist whom he might like to engage in his church. In turn, when he has a revival meeting, the church he has visited can visit him and help him with his attendance during his revival. The visiting pastor is asked to sit on the platform and take part in the service.

Delegations also might be organized from other organizations such as the Boy Scouts and Girl Scouts, plants, factories, stores, Gideons, Christian Business Men, and other groups. All of this helps to reach people with the gospel.

VII. SUNDAY SCHOOL COMMITTEE

We feel the Sunday School is a tremendous opportunity for the winning of souls to Jesus Christ at all times and especially during the revival campaign. Every effort in the world should be made to bring the entire Sunday School under the power and impact of the revival meeting. It is us usually good to start the first Monday night of the campaign with what is called Sunday School Night.

Every department is urged to come and sit together and be recognized with teachers, officers, and pupils. The department with the highest percentage present is given an award. This reaches many boys and girls, men and women, who would not otherwise be reached. In many revival campaigns the Sunday school constituency never hears the evangelist preach. This often times is the result of poor planning and the lack of preparation.

CHAPTER ELEVEN HOW A CHURCH SHOULD CHOSE AND TREAT AN EVANGELIST

TEXT: "**And he gave some apostles and some prophets and some evangelists, and some pastors and teachers**" (Ephesians 4:11).

Notice in God's Word among the five gifted men the Spirit of God has placed in the church is the evangelist. We should remember that the evangelist is a God-called, God-gifted man placed in the Body of Christ to do a special work for the Lord.

In the previous discussion we tried to suggest some things which might be helpful to churches in preparing for a revival campaign and the coming of an evangelist for a special series of services. Again, we repeat, as we said in the previous discussion, we do not assume the step of a Know-It-All. I'm sure there is much about evangelism and church revivals that we do not know, and we are learning as we go along. However, I have felt definitely impressed of the Lord to pass along to my preacher brethren, students preparing for Christian service, and the churches at large a few helpful suggestions which I've picked up along the way. I have made a good many mistakes myself along this line and have learned a few things by trying the wrong method first. I would like to discuss the matter under five headings.

I. THE INVITATION

First of all, I will discuss the invitation to an evangelist. We can thank God that across the country there are a good many capable, Spirit-filled, unselfish, God-called evangelists who are doing a great work for the Lord. I count many of them among my personal friends and pray for them and for their successful ministry in winning the lost for Jesus Christ.

When a church and pastor consider inviting an evangelist to hold a revival campaign, they should first of all prayerfully select and invite an evangelist who has the interest of the church on his heart, who endeavors to win souls to Jesus Christ but will not leave the vineyard in worse shape when he leaves than he found it when he came. An evangelist ought to be a blessing not only to the church and be used of God to the winning of many precious souls, but he ought to be a help and blessing and source of encouragement to the pastor himself and should leave the church not only with souls saved but also in better condition in every way than it was before he came.

He should not do harm to the church that would cause undue worry and concern and burden to the pastor after he is gone. Churches and pastors, I say, should be very prayerful about the selection of an evangelist.

Evangelists should be contacted well in advance so as to work out the most agreeable date for both the church and the evangelist.

II. THE ACCOMMODATION

I know that God-called evangelists are unselfish men. They are not looking for a life of ease. They are not looking for luxuries or comforts. If they were, they certainly would not be in evangelistic work. It would be more comfortable and more luxurious for an evangelist to be home with his family than it would for him to be traveling across the country as a tramp preacher, staying in hotels and homes and places where many times he is not very comfortable.

In order to have an evangelist to be at his best, he should be given a private room in a reputable hotel or motel. I do not think it best under ordinary circumstances for an evangelist to be asked to stay in a home. I know that he would be willing to, but he needs privacy so that he can pray and study and rest and be at his best when the time for the evening meeting comes.

It has been our experience that many times evangelists placed in homes are so busy entertaining and being entertained that they do not have the proper time to study God's Word, to pray, and to rest; and, consequently, they are not at their best and often the meeting is hindered. It is our recommendation that an evangelist be placed in a reputable hotel or motel with a private room so that he can be alone, because much of the time he should be alone if he is to be successful in his ministry.

III. COOPERATION

We have sometimes seen pastors who take the attitude when the evangelist comes, "Well, you are here now. Let's see what you can do." Sometimes pastors do not help and cooperate and work shoulder-to-shoulder with the evangelist. I thank God for those good pastors for whom I've held revival campaigns in the past who were busy during the meeting trying to win every soul they could. They did personal work in the meetings. They stood by the evangelist. They encouraged him. They earnestly prayed for him and with him. They did everything to make him feel welcome and happy and wanted and appreciated. Do not insist that he always do things "your way" or "as it has always been done in the past."

IV. CONSIDERATION

There are a number of small items that ought to be taken into consideration when an evangelist is asked to come to a meeting. Remember, he is away from his family and spends many lonely hours. He should be allowed the privilege of calling his home at least once at the expense of the church. He should be allowed to eat his meals when and where he so chooses. Many of the men of God are carrying such heavy burdens and have been in the work so long that they cannot eat many of the things they are expected to eat.

They should be allowed to select their meals in a good restaurant and eat when and where they would like. It is our personal opinion that an evangelist should not be asked to be calling every day along with the pastor. This does not mean that an evangelist is not willing to do personal work, he is. He will speak to people he meets everywhere about their souls. Many pastors take an evangelist from morning till night and expect him, in a week or two weeks' time, to help them to do the visitation work that the pastor should have been doing all the year. This is not considerate. An evangelist does not come to do pastoral work. He comes to win the lost; he comes, to edify and encourage the believer.

V. REMUNERATION

This is a touchy subject with many pastors but it should not be so. The Bible says "**A laborer is worthy of his hire**" and "**Muzzle not the ox that treadeth out the corn.**"

Many pastors are most inconsiderate in the matter of remuneration for God-called evangelists. For instance, if an evangelist comes to your church to conduct a revival campaign and starts on Sunday and closes on Sunday, holding an eight-day meeting, he has given you two weeks of his time. This should be taken into consideration. He should have a generous offering, for it is his only income. These men of God are dependent upon the churches for their livelihood.

It is our conviction that many times churches have been most inconsiderate of these God-called evangelists. Their traveling needs, their hotel expense, and their food should be taken care of by the church over and above the love offering. An evangelist has many needs and expenses that the average Christian has never thought of, and the church should do everything in its power to give a generous and liberal offering for the evangelist. It has been our experience that God richly blesses the pastor and the church that will go all out to care for the needs of the evangelist, that kind of church is blessed and prospered and experiences growth.

On the other hand, I have seen churches that have been stingy with evangelists remain small and struggle for their needs and have trouble of all kinds.

Sometimes pastors feel envious of an evangelist for securing a love offering which often amounts to more than the pastor's weekly salary. This ought not to be. No pastor should be jealous for what a servant of God gets in his church for a week or two weeks of revival services.

Sometimes pastors, by their attitude toward the evangelist in being stingy with him, teach their people to be the same. That is why many pastors do not have their needs supplied by the church. Through the years they have been selfish and little in this matter of remuneration for God's itinerant servants, and thus they have unconsciously taught their churches to deal with them the same way.

Remember, Jesus said, "**It is more blessed to give than to receive**," and "**Give and it shall be given unto you; good measure, pressed down, shaken together and running over shall men give into your bosom for with the same measure that you meet withal it shall be measured to you again**" (Luke 6:38).

Some of the things to remember in the matter of remunerating the evangelist are:

1. His traveling expense in coming to you should be cared for by the Church.
2. Any time the evangelist takes off during the year to be with his family such as at Christmas time, etc., he will be without an income.
3. Any unavoidable cancellations of meetings during the year leave him this time open without income.
4. His operating expenses are usually greater than those of the pastor by nature of his type of ministry.
5. God's people usually want to give to an evangelist and they respect their pastor for respecting the needs of God-called evangelists.
6. Remember, dear fellow pastors, jealousy on our part of the income or popularity of an evangelist is usually detected by our people.
7. Prayerfully put yourself in his shoes and him in yours and ask yourself, "How would I like to be remunerated and treated if I were an evangelist?"

CHAPTER TWELVE HOW AN EVANGELIST SHOULD TREAT A CHURCH AND PASTOR

We have discussed "How a Church Should Prepare for a Revival Campaign" and "How a Church Should Treat an Evangelist." Now we wish to discuss "How an Evangelist Should Treat a Church and Pastor."

A good Scripture for this is Colossians 3:17, "**And whatsoever ye do in word or deed, do all in the name of the Lord Jesus.**" This, of course, is a good standard for every work of the child of God. In Christian work things should be done in the name of the Lord and for the glory of God.

Again we would like to repeat in regard to this discussion that we in no sense of the word presume to have all the answers on these matters. We are hoping and praying that as evangelists, pastors, and believers in all walks of life think on these things that other ideas will come to their mind which will be helpful along these subjects.

There are seven statements that could be made about how an evangelist should treat the church.

I. HE SHOULD NOT FEEL THAT ALL THE RESULTS ARE BECAUSE OF HIS EFFORTS

The evangelist should remember that the faithful pastor has been there, in most cases, sowing the seed, the Word of God, for a good many years. In addition to this, the people have been praying and working and witnessing, trying to bring conviction upon the hearts and lives of the unsaved for many months and, in some instances, for many years before he ever came.

He should not assume the egotistical attitude that all the results achieved in a given campaign are the direct results of his own ministry. He should remember that Jesus said in John 4:35-38, "**Say not ye, There are yet four months, and then cometh harvest? Behold, I say unto you, Lift up your eyes, and look on the fields; for they are white already to harvest. And he that reapeth receiveth wages, and gathereth fruit unto life eternal: that both he that soweth and he that reapeth may rejoice together. And herein is that saying true, One soweth, and another reapeth. I sent you to reap that whereon ye bestowed no labour: other men laboured, and ye are entered into their labours."

Jesus mentions several important items in this brief passage.

- The fields are white unto harvest, and there are many to be won.
- He that sows and he that reaps ought to rejoice together and share the joy and the reward of the souls won.
- Many times preachers reap results when they actually did no sowing themselves.
- Sowing and reaping are equally important.

II. HE SHOULD NOT DWELL ON NONESSENTIALS AND CONTROVERSIAL SUBJECTS

An evangelist in a revival campaign should not dwell upon the nonessentials and controversial subjects which are not necessary to the edification of the church and the winning of the lost for Jesus Christ. He should not ride hobbies, so to speak, and speak on controversial subjects which are irrelevant to the work of soul-winning. We do not mean by this, of course, in any sense of the word that an evangelist should ever compromise his convictions in his ministry because of lack of agreement on the part of the pastor with what he believes and preaches. However, it is often the case that an evangelist will get into nonessential matters and very controversial subjects that cause contention and division in the church, and disastrous results follow long after the evangelist is gone.

He should stick to the business of preaching the Word, the gospel, the good tidings, the good news that Christ died to save sinners, of winning people to Christ, and of edifying the body of our Lord.

III. HE SHOULD AT ALL TIMES BE LOYAL TO THE PASTOR

It is our conviction that an evangelist should at all times be loyal to the pastor. This does not mean that he is called upon to condone and approve any mistakes the pastor might have made; but in every revival campaign there are malcontents and the unhappy ones who, if allowed to do so, would complain to the evangelist about their disagreements with the pastor. No evangelist should ever allow a member of a local church to complain and talk about the pastor without the pastor's being present. The evangelist under all circumstances should feel that it is his God-given duty to be loyal to the man of God whom the Lord has placed in that place. Many times, if evangelists side in with those who are discontented, they cause much trouble and disaster in the church long after they are gone.

IV. HE SHOULD REMEMBER THAT ALL EVANGELISTS WILL BE JUDGED BY HIM

The whole work of evangelism has often been hurt by needless mistakes and unnecessary blunders on the part of the evangelist. Every evangelist should remember that the whole divine profession of evangelism and every God-called evangelist will be judged by the way he conducts himself, by his very appearance and attitude and the nature of his work.

V. HE SHOULD NOT PRESUME UPON THE GENEROSITY AND THE LIBERALITY OF THE PEOPLE OF GOD

A complaint often given by pastors is that evangelists sometimes secure the names and addresses of their people while conducting a revival campaign; and then in the months and years which follow, they write back promoting their own work, asking for contributions, and thus hinder and hurt the work of the local church. We feel that this is wrong on the part of the evangelist. No evangelist should ever presume upon the generosity and the liberality of the people of God who love him and admire him and become attached to him during a revival campaign because of the work of the Lord which he is doing.

VI. HE SHOULD BE CAREFUL IN MONEY MATTERS

We have always been a strong proponent of good, generous, liberal offerings for the evangelist in a revival campaign. We feel that a church should go all out and do its very best and give a generous offering to the God-called evangelist. We've mentioned this before. However, when evangelists express disappointment in regard to the amount of the offering when the people have done their best, harm is done to the whole cause of evangelism in the matter of money.

The evangelist should be very careful, also, about the money he spends as far as meals, lodging, and other expenses which are to be charged to the church. Just because the church has agreed to foot the bill is no excuse for him to be reckless and careless in the matter of spending money for meals, lodging, phone bills, etc.

VII. HE SHOULD AVOID THE APPEARANCE OF EVIL

At all times the evangelist should avoid the appearance of evil. His counseling with individuals should always be done in the church and in the pastor's study with the pastor present. He should never allow people to come to his room for a private conference because this brings reproach upon the Name of the Lord. The evangelist is under constant scrutiny of hundreds of people. He should be sure that his personal appearance, his personal conduct, his mannerisms, and his conversation are above reproach at all times, both in the pulpit and out of it.

Printed in Great Britain
by Amazon

Facing
Bjorn Borg

By Scoop Malinowski

Cover Artwork By Alberto Ramirez Suarez

Copyright 2022 Scoop Malinowski

All rights reserved.

IISBN: 9798750082452

CONTRIBUTORS

Andre Agassi
Roy Barth
Manuel Orantes
Horace Reid
Mark Wagner
Roger Taylor
Hans Gildemeister
Rob Koenig
Brian Gottfried
Jimmy Gleason
Noel Callaghan
Reid Sheftall
Walter Redondo
Ivan Lendl
Bob Billingworth
Bunner Smith
Chris Lewis
Brian Sidney Parrott
Rod Laver
Bettina Bunge
Larry Denyes
Joe Yanagisawa
Steve Carter
Gerard Faulkner
Anonymous
Howard Winitsky
Bill Lloyd
John Williams Hayes
Jim Tarsy
Swedish newspaper reporter
Johan Kriek
Stefan Edberg
John McEnroe
Steve Siebold

Harold Solomon
Donald Dell
Lisa Bonder-Kerkorian
Gene Mayer
Mats Torngren
Erik Siklos
Ernesto Ruiz-Bry
Nicolai Herlofson
Jimmy Connors
Guillermo Vilas
John Lloyd
Steve Krulevitz
Stan Smith
Mohammad Ali-Akbar
David Bush
Lennart Bergelin
Mariana Simonescu
Rayni Fox-Borinsky
Corrado Barazzutti
Marcos Manqueros
Andrei Cherkasov
Emilion Benfele Alvarez
Jorge Andrew
Henner Lenhardt
Tim Taylor
Michel Loutchmaninoff
Liz Kennedy
Gilad Bloom
Phil Secada
Bunner Smith
Arthur Ashe
Ilie Nastase
Reno Manne
Juan Coronel

The Viking from Sweden was both beauty and beast personified on the tennis court... an unstoppable force at Roland Garros and Wimbledon, capturing eleven majors combined in Paris and London before the age of 26. One of the most recognizable figures in the history of sport won 64 singles titles overall.

Bjorn Rune Borg was born on June 6, 1956 in Stockholm, Sweden. He was the only child of Rune Borg, an electrician, and Margaretha. Legend has it that Borg became intrigued by tennis because of a golden racquet his father had won from competing in a table tennis tournament. Young Bjorn used the racquet to begin playing tennis which he excelled at. Physically gifted and athletic with a strong upper body and the footspeed and endurance of a sprinter and distance runner, Borg would employ a heavy top spin style of play on both his forehand and two-handed backhand strikes. By age thirteen he could beat the best of Sweden's under eighteen players.

At age fifteen in 1972, Borg made his Davis Cup debut for Sweden and captain Lennart Bergelin, who later became his primary coach in the professional ranks. Borg defeated veteran Onny Parun of New Zealand in five sets. Later in 1972, Borg won junior Wimbledon, defeating Great Britain's Buster Mottram from 2-5 down in the third set. In December of 1972, Borg won the Orange Bowl, besting Vitas Gerulaitis in straight sets.

Borg turned pro in 1973 and quickly made an impact, reaching the final of Monte Carlo, losing to Ilie Nastase. He reached the fourth round of Roland Garros (lost to Adriano Panatta) and quarterfinals of Wimbledon (lost to Roger Taylor in five sets). Borg would later reach the fourth round at US Open and the finals in San Francisco, Buenos Aires and Stockholm and finish 1973 ranked no. 18 in the world.

In 1974, Borg competed at the Australian Open for the only time in his career. He lost to eventual finalist Phil Dent in the third round. Borg's first ATP singles title was won in January 1974 in New Zealand. This triumph sparked more success - in February Borg added his second title in London and in March a third championship in Sao Paulo. Still not yet eighteen, Borg won the Italian Open in June. Two weeks later, Borg became the youngest man to win the French Open by defeating Manuel Orantes in five sets.

If thou wouldst be an artist, foresake all sadness and care, save for thy art. Let thou soul be as a mirror, which reflects all objects, all movements and colors, remaining itself unmoved and clear... --Leonardo Da Vinci

Borg's 11 Grand Slam Title Draws

1974 Roland Garros

Finals	Manuel Orantes	W 26 67 60 61 61
SF	Harold Solomon	W 64 26 62 61
QF	Raul Ramirez	W 62 57 46 62 63
R16	Erik Van Dillen	W 06 63 63 57 63
R32	Jean-Loup Rouyer	W 64 62 60
R64	Toma Ovici	W 61 61
R128	Jean-Francois Caujolle	W 46 60 64

1975 Roland Garros

Finals	Guillermo Vilas	W 62 63 64
SF	Adriano Panatta	W 64 16 75 64
QF	Harold Solomon	W 61 75 64
R16	Stan Smith	W 62 63 60
R32	Jiri Hrebec	W 61 61 61
R64	Peter Szoke	W 61 61
R128	Norman Holmes	W 62 63

1976 Wimbledon

Finals	Ilie Nastase	W 64 62 97
SF	Roscoe Tanner	W 64 98 64
QF	Guillermo Vilas	W 63 60 62
R16	Brian Gottfried	W 62 62 75
R32	Colin Dibley	W 64 64 64
R64	Marty Riessen	W 62 62 64
R128	David Lloyd	W 63 63 61

1977 Wimbledon

Finals	Jimmy Connors	W 36 62 61 57 64
SF	Vitas Gerulaitis	W 64 36 63 36 86
QF	Ilie Nastase	W 60 86 63
R16	Wojtek Fibak	W 75 64 62
R32	Nikola Pilic	W 97 75 63
R64	Mark Edmondson	W 36 79 62 64 61
R128	Antonio Zugarelli	W 64 62 97

1978 Roland Garros

Finals	Guillermo Vilas	W 61 61 63
SF	Corrado Barazzutti	W 60 61 60
QF	Raul Ramirez	W 63 63 60
R16	Roscoe Tanner	W 62 64 76
R32	Paolo Bertolucci	W 60 62 62
R64	Rick Fagel	W 60 61 60
R128	Eric Deblicker	W 61 61 61

1978 Wimbledon

Finals	Jimmy Connors	W 62 62 63
SF	Tom Okker	W 64 64 64
QF	Sandy Mayer	W 75 64 63
R16	Geoff Masters	W 62 64 86
R32	Jaime Fillol	W 64 62 68 64
R64	Peter McNamara	W 62 62 64
R128	Victor Amaya	W 89 61 16 63 63

1979 Roland Garros

Finals	Victor Pecci	W 63 61 67 64
SF	Vitas Gerulaitis	W 62 61 60
QF	Hans Gildemeister	W 64 61 75
R16	Gilles Moretton	W 75 64 62
R32	Raymond Moore	W 63 61 60
R64	Tom Gullikson	W 63 76 57 64
R128	Tomas Smid	W 61 57 64 64

1979 Wimbledon

Finals	Roscoe Tanner	W 67 61 36 63 64
SF	Jimmy Connors	W 62 63 62
QF	Tom Okker	W 62 61 63
R16	Brian Teacher	W 64 57 64 75
R32	Hank Pfister	W 64 61 63
R64	Vijay Amritraj	W 26 64 46 76 62
R128	Tom Gorman	W 36 64 75 61

1980 Roland Garros

Finals	Vitas Gerulaitis	W 64 61 62
SF	Harold Solomon	W 62 62 60
QF	Corrado Barazzutti	W 60 63 63
R16	Balazs Taroczy	W 62 62 60
R32	Pascal Portes	W 63 60 61
R64	Andres Gomez	W 62 62 61
R128	Alvaro Fillol	W 63 61 64

1980 Wimbledon

Finals	John McEnroe	W 16 75 63 67 86
SF	Brian Gottfried	W 62 46 62 60
QF	Gene Mayer	W 75 63 75
R16	Balazs Taroczy	W 61 75 62
R32	Rod Frawley	W 64 67 61 75
R64	Shlomo Glickstein	W 63 61 75
R128	Ismail El Shafei	W 63 64 64

1981 Roland Garros

Finals	Ivan Lendl	W 61 46 62 36 61
SF	Victor Pecci	W 64 64 75
QF	Balazs Taroczy	W 63 63 62
R16	Terry Moor	W 60 60 61
R32	Paul Torre	W 62 61 62
R64	Cassio Motta	W 61 75 60
R128	Jose Lopez-Maeso	W 62 62 62

> A tennis player can create more than an artist and with as much satisfaction.
>
> — **Maria Bueno**

> The strongest man on Earth is he who stands most alone.
>
> — **Henrik Ibsen**

> Silence alone is great. All else is weakness.
>
> — **DeVigny**

FACING
BJORN BORG

Andre Agassi: I hit a few balls with my idol Bjorn Borg when I was eight years old. At the Alan King tournament (at Caesars Palace in Las Vegas). My father got me a job as ballboy. He cajoled most of the top pros to hit a few balls with me, Connors, Nastase, Borg. Some were more willing than others. I remember Borg acted as if there was nowhere else he'd rather be.

To Don

FACING
BJORN BORG

Roy Barth: I played Bjorn on the center court at the 1973 US Open in Forest Hills, New York on grass. We started at 3:00pm with the temperature on the court at 106 degrees. I was twenty-five years old playing on my favorite surface - grass. He was seventeen and a rising star. At sixteen, the year before, he lost to Roy Emerson in a close five set match. I had him two sets to love, break point, his second serve at four all. I missed a backhand return by one inch. He went on to win the set 7-5, the 4th set, 6-2. After 3 1/2 hours and at 2 all I got cramps in both legs. In the third and fourth sets he ran like a deer. The more I made him run, the better he played. The heat didn't seem to bother him. He was calm throughout the whole match, showing no emotion. He's truly a great person and player.

Needless to say, in the fifth set at 2-2, I lost the next four games in ten minutes. Bjorn went on to upset Arthur Ashe and reached the quarterfinals... the rest is history.

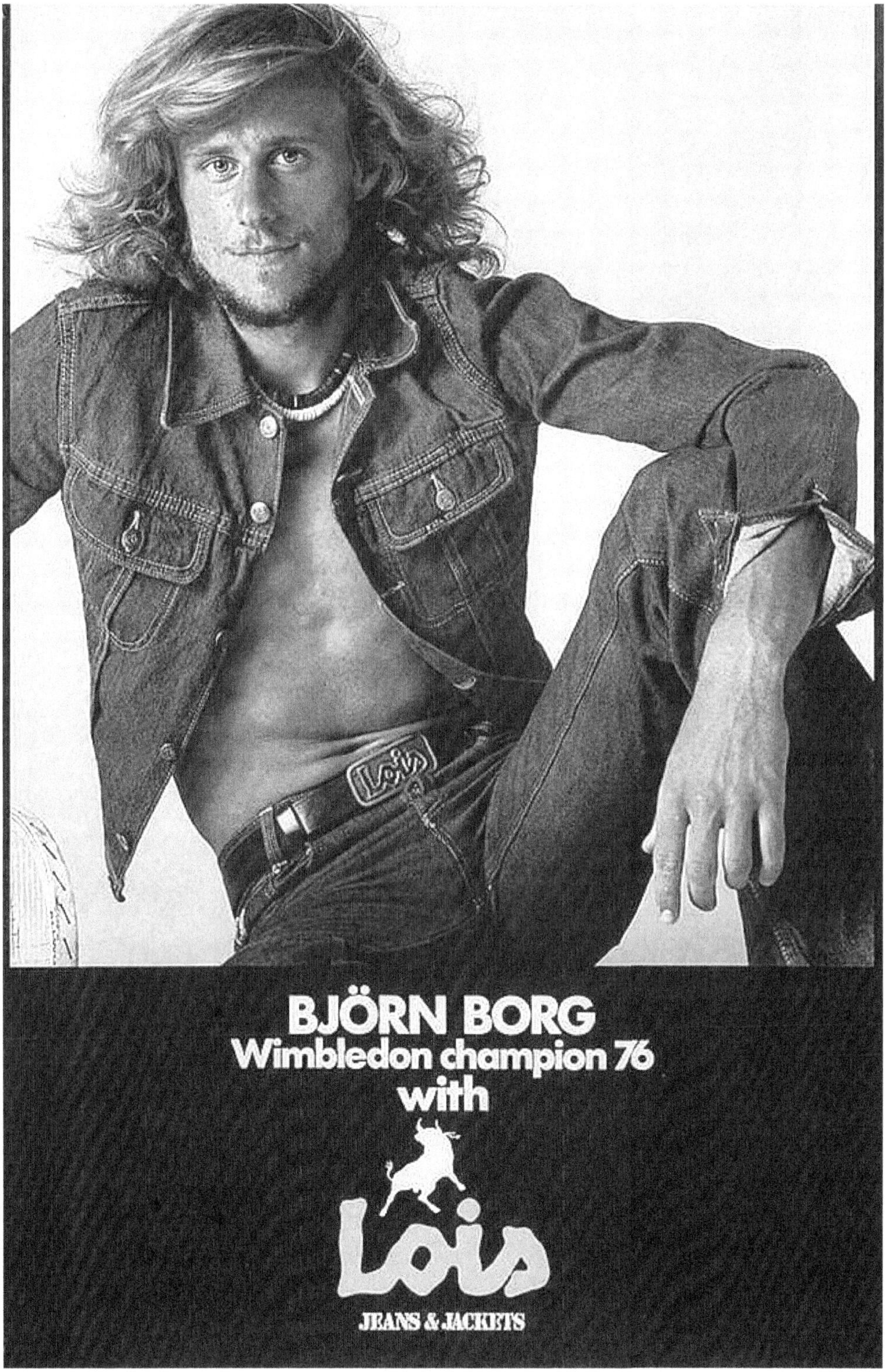
BJÖRN BORG
Wimbledon champion 76
with
Lois
JEANS & JACKETS

FACING
BJORN BORG

Manuel Orantes: Borg is a different story. You look on his face for emotion and there is nothing.

KING OF WATERPROOF WATCHES
SWITZERLAND
Mido
O relógio de classe que atende às mais altas exigências.
Um campeão como Björn Borg é a pessoa ideal para falar em nome de todos que possuem um relógio Mido Ocean Star.
Mido Ocean Star é elegante, esportivo e tem impermeabilidade total, garantida pelo sistema Aquadura tornando-se, por isso mesmo, o relógio ideal para as pessoas mais exigentes.
Björn Borg
QUARTZ

FACING
BJORN BORG

Horace Reid: Back in my day, I would be amazed at how picky some guys were and had a memory of watching Bjorn Borg pick up some freshly strung racquets. He would just hit them against his hand and if it didn't feel right, he would just give it back to the stringer to do over. I was dying inside, knowing that a brand new set of gut strings didn't even have a single hit on them and they were just gonna get cut out!

ADVERTISEMENT

THIS SPECIAL 24-PAGE ADVERTISING INSERT RECORDS IN WORDS AND PICTURES THE NINE TIMES THAT BJORN BORG TRIED BUT FAILED TO WIN THE U.S. OPEN TOURNAMENT.

U.S. OPEN TENNIS AND BJORN BORG

FACING
BJORN BORG

Mark Wagner: Had the cool pleasure to hit with Borg once at Queens. That was a fun day, but what I remember was his grips. They were a massive 5, unlike my 4 1/2. They were like baseball bats, not tennis racquets. He sure was great with them. Best guy I ever played.

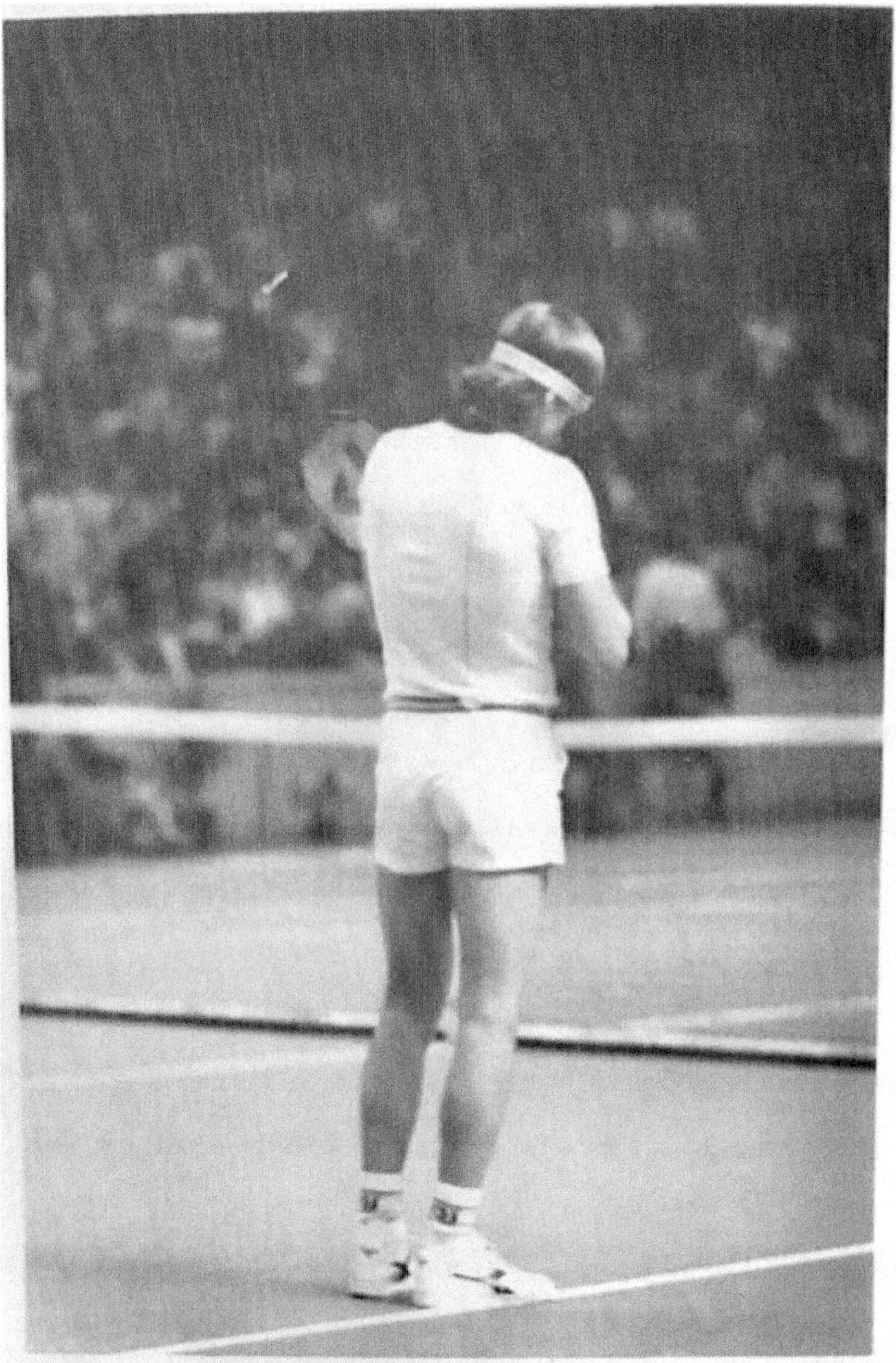

FACING
BJORN BORG

Roger Taylor: I had an amazing match at Wimbledon with Bjorn Borg, who was seventeen at the time. I was about 32, so we were at different ends of the game. He was always a good player. And he was a senior player at the French Championships as young as fourteen. And years ago you didn't have to have a world ranking to get into the tournament. You were nominated by your association. So he was nominated. And he played Davis Cup when he was fifteen. I'm building him up because I managed to beat him [smiles]. He played Davis Cup at fifteen. And I don't think he lost a match. So at seventeen, he was a good player.

We got into this incredible match on Center Court. And five sets creates these matches. I was behind two sets to one. And I came back. And so I lead 5-1 in the fifth set. And Bjorn caught up and got me to five-all. Then I broke serve for 6-5. And then I served for the match. I got the match point. I'm left-handed, so I'm serving from the ad court. And I served a swinging serve which, unfortunately, was just out. But the chair umpire called, 'Game, set and match, Taylor.' And I was sort of turning away - because I knew it was out. A centimenter - but you know it was out. I was just turning back to serve again. And the umpire called it again, 'Game, set and match, Taylor.' So I said, No, no, it was out. So I turned back to serve and I lost the point [smiles]. So everyone is like, What is happening? So I went back to deuce. And then I managed to win the next two points. So I won the match.

The lefty Brit won two US Open doubles titles (1971, 1972) and in singles reached the semis at Wimbledon three times. He won six ATP singles titles and nine more in doubles. Taylor's best singles ranking was no. 11 in 1973.

Head to head series tied at 1-1

1975 Stockholm Indoor Hard   R32   Borg 60 64

1973 Wimbledon Outdoor Grass QF   Taylor 61 68 36 63 75

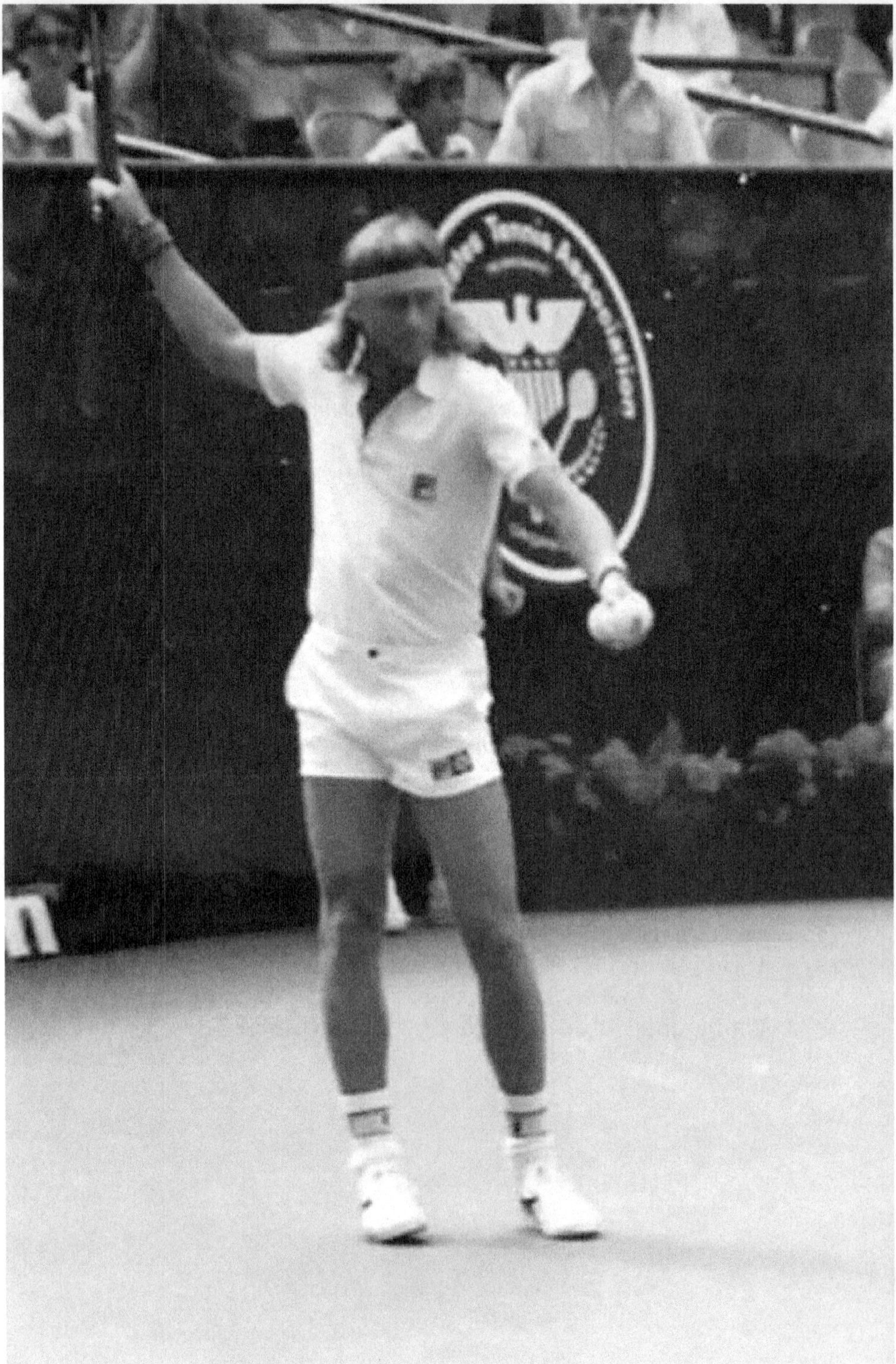

FACING
BJORN BORG

Hans Gildemeister: I have very good memories of Bjorn Borg. I played him many times. Great person. He was very polite, very quiet, and never had any problems with anyone. I remember I lost to him in 1979 at Roland Garros quarterfinal and in WCT Canada that same year. I beat him one time, a four-players event in Santiago, Chile. I won against Vitas Gerulaitis in the final and I beat Borg in two sets. I played one of my best matches to beat Borg 64 63. It was February 1980. The four players were Peter Fleming vs Vitas and me against Borg, the winners played the finals. I played with McEnroe two weeks earlier, also in Santiago exhibition, I lost in four sets.

Question: Were you mistaken for Borg a lot? You have a similar look and face...

Hans Gildemeister: Yes, my wife got confused once in the elevator in

Paris at the French Open in the hotel. I was better looking [smiles].

Hans Gildemeister, from Chile, won four ATP singles titles and achieved a career high ranking of no. 12. In doubles he won 23 titles and reached no. 5 in the world.

Borg won the head to head series 2-0

1979 WCT Challenge Cup Canada Outdoor Hard RR Borg 62 63

1979 Roland Garros Outdoor Clay QF Borg   64 61 75

Bjorn Borg with John William Hayes

FACING
BJORN BORG

Robbie Koenig: My first memory of tennis is watching tennis. It's gotta be Bjorn Borg, Borg winning that Wimbledon final in 1980 against McEnroe. Also, Mats Wilander beating Ivan Lendl, I think it was the final of the U.S. Open (1988). Those two matches in particular, really sparked my interest in the game, Scoop. That's when I really wanted to be out and hit balls all day long and be like those guys. They were my inspirations.

A doubles specialist from South Africa, Koenig won five ATP doubles titles and was once ranked no. 28 in the world.

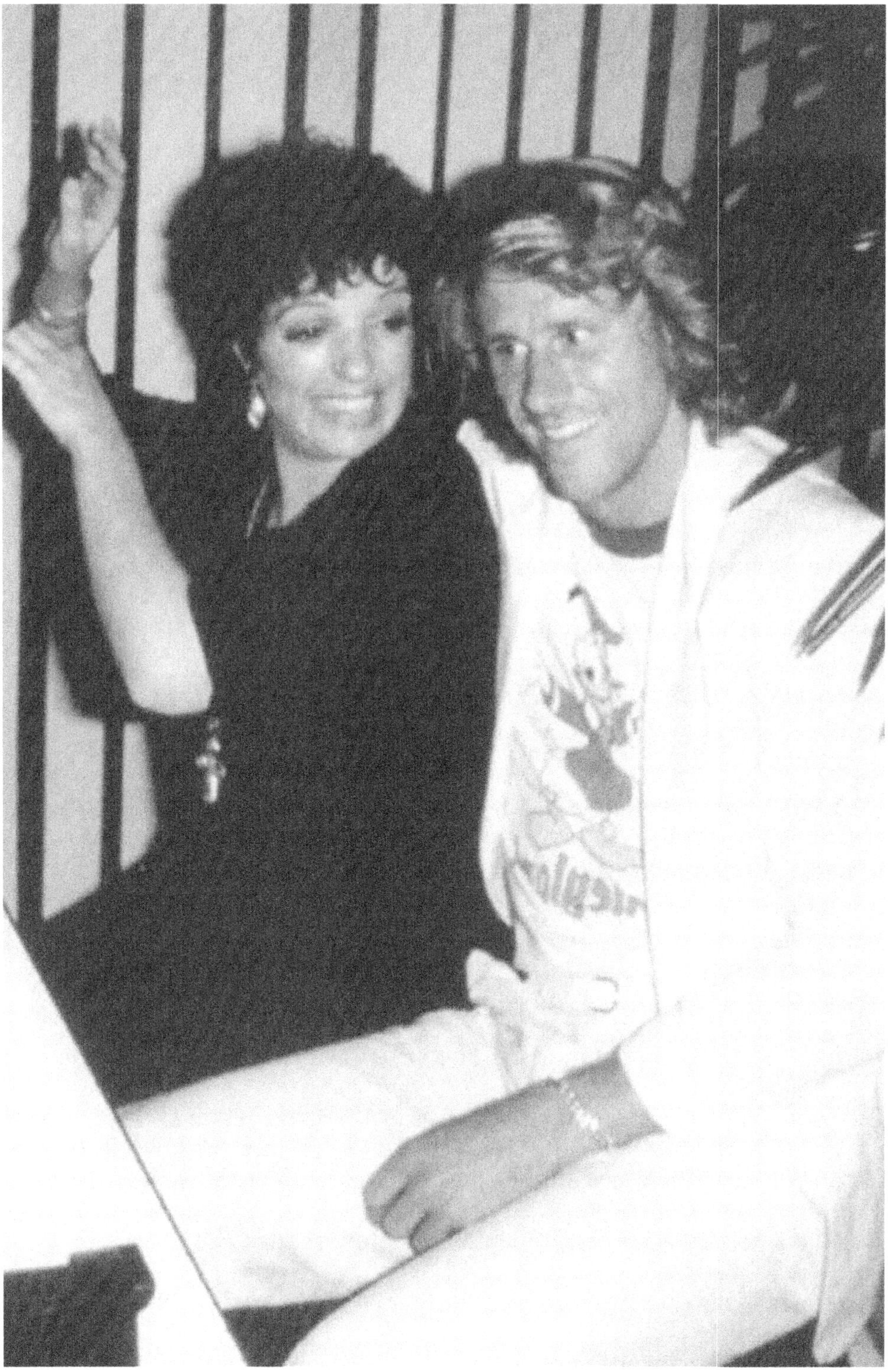

FACING
BJORN BORG

Brian Gottfried: It was always a great experience to play Bjorn. You always knew there wouldn't be any shenanigans or anything other than playing a hard, fair tennis match. I played him many times - once was in 1976 in the round of 16 at the US Open when it was at Forest Hills on clay. I had two sets to love and a break in the third and still didn't think I was going to win. Guess what? I didn't. But it was a match that turned my career around, in that I finally had the confidence in myself to believe I belonged at that level.

I also played him, at least twice, at Wimbledon, during his five winning years. I lost once in the fourth round in 1976 which was the first year he won. Then I lost to him in the semis in 1980, the year he beat Johnny Mac in the finals after losing that great fourth set breaker. I lost in four sets. On grass he came into the net more than he did on clay, but he still played a lot from the baseline. And back in the 1970's and 1980's the courts weren't as good and as hard as they are today, so there were more bad bounces. But with his speed and quickness he was able to still play from the baseline. It always seemed like he never got a bad bounce on his side of the court. That made it difficult for me on grass since I tried to serve and volley both serves. Usually my points were very short on grass. But against Borg I was forced to play differently than I had played in the matches and the weeks leading up to Wimbledon. I had to try to stay back a little more because it was difficult for me to serve and volley on my second serve. So I was in a quandary. Which uncomfortable thing should I do, serve and volley on second serves or stay back on grass? So that was a real challenge for me.

Also his nerves and his ability to raise his game and play at a higher level at critical times of a match made him special. There was usually a match or two each year at Wimbledon where someone would have a lead on him but wouldn't beat him. I remember Victor Amaya, Vijay Amritraj and Mark Edmondson had opportunities but didn't win. Bjorn was always able to believe in himself and raise his game when he had to.

These are some of my memories of Bjorn and my times playing him. Oh, I completely forgot your question (about the two times Brian managed to beat him). Stockholm 1976, when I won that match the thing I remember most was the dead silence - a couple thousand Swedes watching and not one of them made a sound when the match was over. I guess they were as surprised as I was. La Costa 1977 - he hated to play on hard courts and it was my best surface and I think he walked on the court thinking it was going to be a tough day. 1977 was my best year. Personally, I think he remembered that I had him two sets to love at the US Open the previous year and he felt sorry for me.

Distinguished by his relentless work ethic and intelligent strategizing, the curly-haired American won 25 singles, 54 doubles, and three Grand Slam doubles titles. His best efforts fell agonizingly short of legendary grandeur - the 1977 Roland Garros final loss to Vilas and career best ranking of no. 3. His ATP career singles record was 702-330.

Borg won head to head series 9-2

1980   Wimbledon Outdoor Grass SF Borg 62 46 62 60

1979   New Orleans WCT Indoor Carpet QF Borg 61 57 63

1978   Pepsi Grand Slam FL Outdoor Clay SF Borg 62 64

1977   Masters NY Indoor Carpet   RR   Gottfried W/O

1977   Denver CO Indoor Carpet F Borg 75 62

1977   Carlsbad CA   Outdoor Hard SF Gottfried 61 61

1977   MemphisTN   Indoor Carpet F   Borg 64 63 46 75

1976   Stockholm Sweden   Indoor Hard   QF   Gottfried 62 46 76

1976   US Open   Outdoor Clay   R16   Borg 67 36 64 64 62

1976   Wimbledon Outdoor Grass   R16   Borg 62 62 75

1974   Stockholm   Indoor Hard R16   Borg 64 61

1974   Indianapolis Outdoor Clay QF Borg 64 36 62

FACING
BJORN BORG

Jimmy Gleason: Borg is my all-time favorite player. Because he played like he was otherworldly, under the greatest pressure didn't miss most times. He's one of the greatest champions of all time. Borg had a real aura about him and he never lost his cool on the court. Loved his battles with Jimmy Connors and John McEnroe.

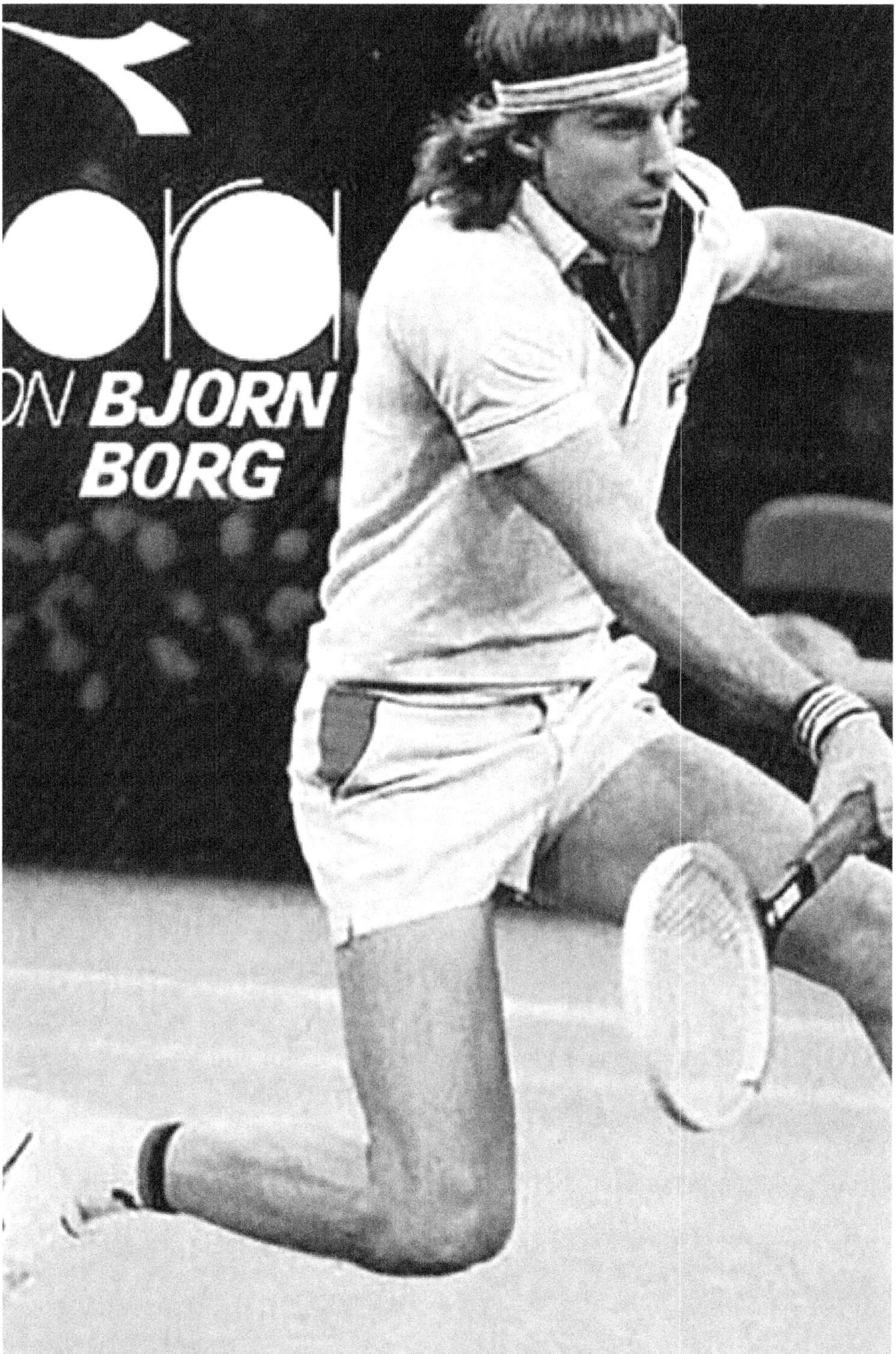
ON BJORN
BORG

FACING
BJORN BORG

Noel Callaghan: I met Borg in 1973. Bjorn was super nice and very quiet and only sixteen when I met him in March, I was still only seventeen. We played a few practice sets and he always 'allowed me' one game per set I guess because he liked me [smiles].

Question: Was it at a junior tournament?

Noel Callaghan: It was in Valencia, Spain ....an early and incredibly strong ATP event with Panatta, Orantes and many more.

Question: What about his game was so difficult for you?

Noel Callaghan: Nothing about his game was difficult for me, I could rally with him all day, the difference was he wouldn't miss. One last thing...... in 1974 I had two wins over Bjorn... firstly in squash ... and secondly in snooker [laughs].

FACING
BJORN BORG

Reid Sheftall: Borg once said: "I never try to hit a winner."

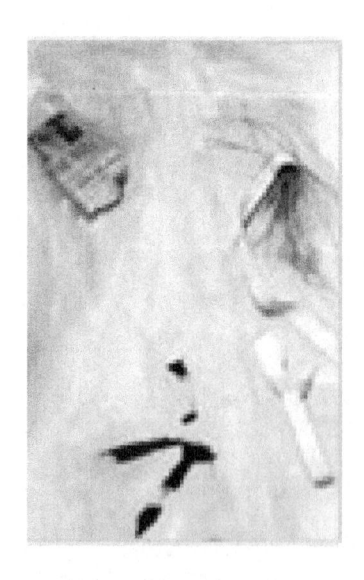

Andres Bella art work.

FACING
BJORN BORG

Walter Redondo: I never really met Borg, I just have memories of being around him on Tour. There was an incident at the US Open in the locker room... there was a separate room in the locker room and he was sitting there by himself. When you would walk by you would experience a sense of confidence and authority. That's something I always remembered. And there was this other experience... where he had to play center court against the No. 1 player from Canada (David Brown) who I happened to be friends with. And I just wanted to see how he was going to respond with the pressure knowing he was playing the No. 1 player of Canada in Toronto. I remember witnessing and sensing Borg (No. 5 in the world at the time) understood the pressure was not on him but rather on the No. 1 player. He understood he just had to make the ball, and that's what he did, he won the match (first round, 60 62 in 1975) knowing he had one job and he executed it.

The San Diego, CA former pro accomplished a career best ATP singles ranking of no. 226 and he reached round of 16 in Wimbledon doubles.

FACING
BJORN BORG

Ivan Lendl: Bjorn didn't stay on the main regular tour long enough to have a serious competitive history with me (though they did play eight times between 1979 and 1981 with Borg winning six of the eight duels including the 1981 Roland Garros final 61 46 62 36 61). But I'll tell you this: he didn't appear as intimidating as McEnroe or Connors because he was a master at controlling and hiding his emotions. But if you weren't at the top of your game against Bjorn, he would quietly and relentlessly dominate you.

Four Grand Slam final failures could not discourage this determined Czech challenger who finally became champion at Roland Garros in 1984, overcoming a two set deficit to McEnroe. The avid fitness devotee carefully constructed himself into a formidable force who collected seven more majors and 94 singles titles overall and over $21 million in prize money.

Borg won head to head series 6-2

1981   Stuttgart Outdoor Clay F   Borg 16 76 62 64

1981   Roland Garros Outdoor Clay F   Borg 61 46 62 36 61

1980   Masters NY Indoor Carpet F Borg 64 62 62

1980   Basel Indoor Hard F   Lendl 63 62 57 06 64

1980   Toronto Outdoor Hard F Lendl 46 54 RET

1980   Monte Carlo WCT Outdoor Clay R16   Borg 62 62

1979   CZ vs. SWE - B FINAL Czech Rep Outdoor Clay RR   Borg 64 75 62

1979   Toronto Outdoor Hard SF Borg 63 61

FACING
BJORN BORG

Bob Billingworth: Borg was the reason I gave up baseball for tennis in high school.

FACING
BJORN BORG

Bunner Smith: Watching Bjorn at fifteen at the Orange Bowl ... We all knew he would go on to be great... One of the best ever .... Love to see a prime career match on red clay between Borg and Nadal......five sets...11-9 in the fifth.

I played him at Orange Bowl 18s. It was nearly 45-46 years ago! Miami ... I grew up in Florida and had played lots of future top players... Harold Solomon, Brian Gottfried, Billy Martin. Billy never missed. But, Borg was a totally different level. From what I remember, his forehand was huge and I never got passed by anyone so much ever as I did by Borg that day. Borg rarely if ever made an unforced error. Everyone knew he was special and expected him to be a future top pro. Best ever on clay until Rafa came along. He was the best player I ever played.

He was young, younger than me and very quiet on the court. He had the long hair and the headband then too. I don't remember much conversation. From what I remember he was quiet and all business on the court. I Watched him play him so many times over those years. His on court focus was always as good as anyone ever... stoic!

FACING
BJORN BORG

Chris Lewis: "I first saw Bjorn play in early 1974, when, as a teenager, he won the New Zealand Open - on fast grass, beating Onny Parun in the final. It was a time when Bjorn Borg emerged as a seventeen-year-old superstar who required heavy police protection at Wimbledon to prevent crazed throngs of teenage girls from mobbing him. In one incident, he was attacked on his way to the Wimbledon Village by hundreds of young girls who had him pinned to the ground for a good fifteen minutes before help arrived.

You may not have heard of Onny Parun, but let me assure you, he was an extremely difficult player to beat on grass. He was an Australian Open finalist and two-time Wimbledon quarterfinalist.
Being approximately the same age as Bjorn, and an aspiring player myself, I took a very keen interest in his game. The things that impressed me most were his movement, his incredible passing shots, his consistency, and a

will of steel. You just knew the guy was made of special stuff. In those days, what really made him stand out was his unique style. Nobody was playing with such heavy topspin off both sides, particularly on fast grass courts where penetrating slice approaches - a la Ken Rosewall and Tony Roche - were the order of the day.

I never saw Bjorn play either Ken or Tony, and don't want to imply that he wouldn't have had trouble with them. I suspect he would have as I vaguely remember Bjorn finding Tony a real handful during World Team Tennis one year.

The first, and only, Tour match I played against Bjorn was on clay in the quarters of the Swedish Open in the late 70s. His reputation on clay was already one of invincibility. As I recall, he'd won his first two rounds losing only a couple of games. And combined with the fact that he was on home ground on his favorite surface playing a player who was dating his ex-girlfriend, Swedish player Helena Anliot, I don't need to tell you that I was up for the match.

We played on center court in front of a packed arena. Being a player who, like Bjorn, also kept in good shape, I wasn't at all daunted by the prospect of a grueling physical encounter, something that many players were scared of, especially when they played Bjorn.

It needs to be said that playing a match on slow clay using heavy wooden racquets - Bjorn's were strung at eighty pounds - was no fun if you weren't in shape. And given that consistently hitting winners from the baseline was not an option, if you were to beat Bjorn from the back of the court, the only way to do it was to turn the match into the equivalent of a 10,000 meter race.

And that's pretty much what happened. Without boring you with the details, here's what Bjorn said about the match:

"I played Chris in a tournament in Bastad, Sweden, in 1979 on a slow clay court, and until then I always thought of him as a grass court player. But when we played this game, I couldn't shake him off. I stayed back and hit some good groundstrokes and then they came back just as quickly. Finally, I won 7-6 6-3, but it was a tough match."

A tough match indeed!

It was noted above that Bjorn's resting pulse rate was either in the 30's or 40's - it was the 30's - and that he beat an Olympic 110m hurdles Gold Medalist in a European Superstars 600m event - I think it was Guy Drut - which said a lot for his athleticism and stamina.
As someone who comes from a tradition of great middle distance running

in New Zealand, Peter Snell, John Walker, I know a GREAT athlete when I see one, let alone play one. I can say with virtual certainty that Bjorn would have been able to run 100 meters in around the 11.0 second mark...that's 10 flat for 100 yards, and that he would have been somewhere in the low thirty-minute range for 10k ...and better with specific training. He also was very strong, deceptively so.

Combine those physical attributes with a will of steel and a playing style that was very awkward to counter -- high bouncing, heavily topspun shots if you stayed back, and sharply dipping, vicious crosscourt angles if you came in - don't forget his topspin lob and the difficulty of smashing them with a racquet with the head-size of a pea, and a sweet-spot the size of an amoeba - and what you've got is someone who achieved what Borg achieved.

With the old wooden racquets, believe me, it was virtually impossible to penetrate his game. On clay, nobody could - no one came close - and on grass, well, nobody could either...until John McEnroe came along, with his extraordinary talent.

Although I'm not going to get drawn into any debate as to whether a great player from a former era would beat a great player from a current era, I can't stress enough that it's very easy to drop context... namely, the playing conditions that characterize(d) each era.

For example, I started on the Tour in the mid 1970s with a wooden Wilson Jack Kramer Pro-Staff, switching to a Prince Woodie in 1981 ...was THAT ever a process. And the Prince Graphite, the original grommet-less Classic in '82.

Believe me, today's generation of racquets are so effortless to play with, I can't overstate how much a part technology has played in the evolution of the game.

I'm digressing, but I had the privilege of hitting with Lew Hoad when he visited Harry Hopman at Hop's Academy in Florida many years ago. I also had the privilege of hitting with Rod Laver, and partnering him in a Senior's event in the 1990s. What those guys could do with the old racquets was extraordinary.

Hoad was a bull of a man who could flick those fourteen-ounce tree trunks around as if they were matchsticks. And Rod had such incredible variety. He had a heavyweight game, with an artist's touch. His skill level was McEnroeish, in the sense he could do things that nobody else in his own era could do.

New Zealand's third man to reach a Grand Slam singles final at Wimbledon in 1983, unseeded, also was the first man to compete in a major final using an oversized racquet, manufactured by Prince. Lewis won three singles titles in his career, in Kitzbuhel, Munich and finally Auckland in 1985.

Borg won the head to head series 1-0

1979 Bastad QF Outdoor Clay Borg   76 63

FACING
BJORN BORG

Brian Sidney Parrott: He was, and is still, such a 'cool dude'....broad shoulders, narrow at the hips. The thing I always think about Bjorn Borg is how INCREDIBLY fast he was...he had another gear. I played with Mark Cox of England in a Charity Exhibition in Salem, Oregon for the Women's Assistance League of Salem....against Borg, who was eighteen...it was 1974. It was a lightning fast basketball floor at Willamette University, 3,000, a sellout. I hit a forehand LATE - playing the deuce side - which was hit as hard as I could hit a tennis ball....heading right for the netcord judges head...Borg was out wide...close to the middle....and the split second I hit it...I thought..."this is going to be the greatest shot I ever hit in my life". Not only did Borg GET to it...he volleyed it away...with authority. I thought...Oh My God! How did he POSSIBLY move that fast to cover that ball?

Bjorn Borg is a class person. Another vignette I have with him to share the kind of guy he is.....it was in Seattle in the summer of 1977. I was subbing for Erik van Dillen on the Sea-Port Cascades....and I was also asked to do the halftime interviews for TV...which was going back live into Portland. Borg had played Steve Docherty (Cascades) the night before in Portland and Steve, with his MONSTER serve, won the set. I asked Bjorn to comment on Steve's play....he was very complimentary.... and then I slipped in one more question. "Bjorn....last question, do you have any advice for young players who might be listening?" Without hesitation he said...."It is important that playing tennis is FUN for you. I see too many young Swedes playing but not enjoying it. I played with my friends and then decided to get serious about it." I thought it was such a great answer to a spontaneous question I asked him. Borg is a classy guy....and was SO FAST. It was breathtaking at times to watch his reactions.

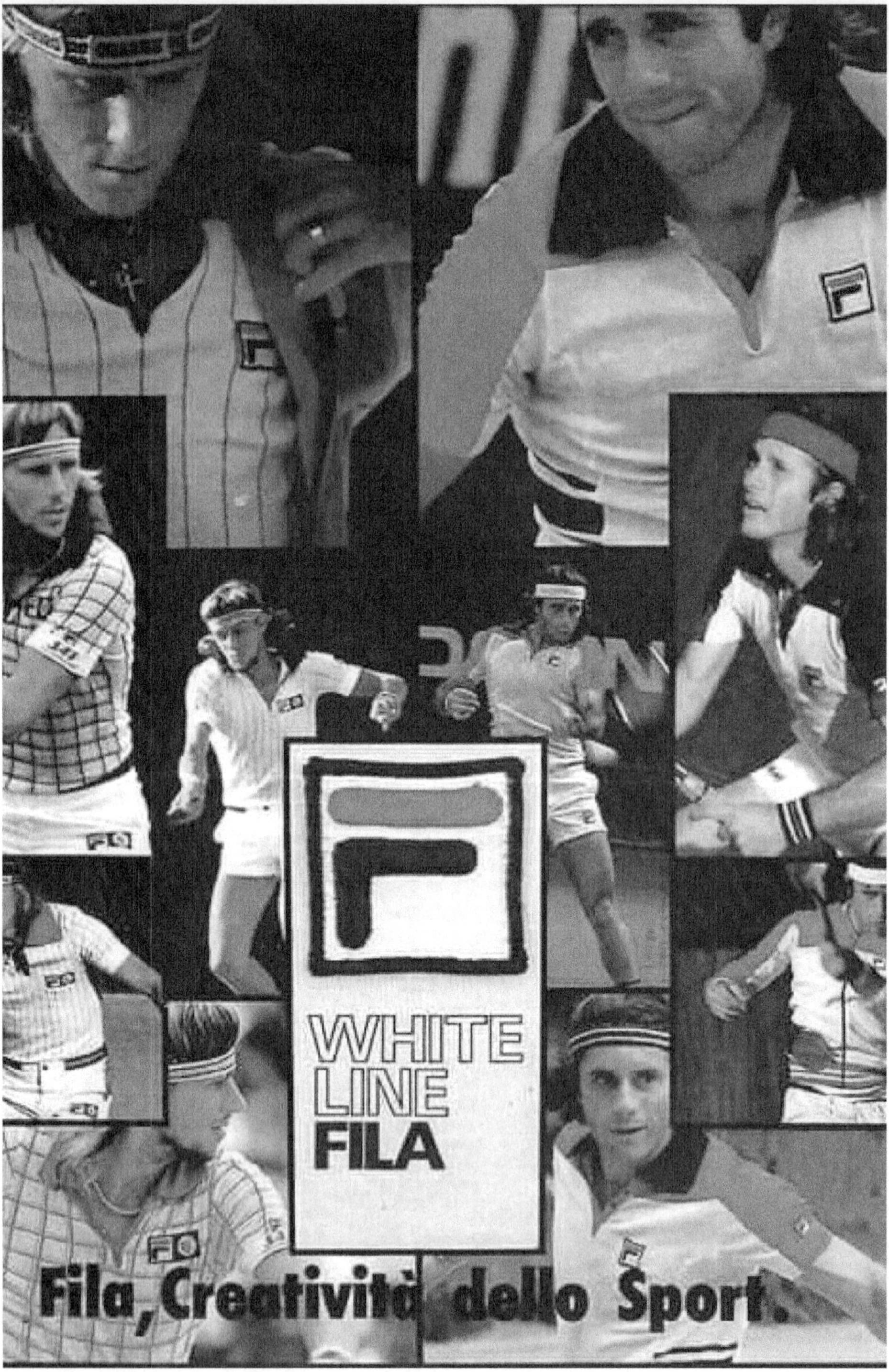
WHITE
LINE
FILA
Fila, Creatività dello Sport.

FACING
BJORN BORG

Rod Laver: In 1975 when I was 37 I dipped into the new generation in matches with the surging Swedish teenager Bjorn Borg (then 19) who was obviously going places. But I wasn't unhappy with my losses to him. It took him five long sets to beat me in the WCT semis at Dallas and four to knock me out of the fourth round at US Open in Forest Hills on green clay. Borg later equaled my eleven Grand Slam singles titles at the 1981 French Open.
(Book excerpt: Rod Laver: Education Of A Tennis Player)

The Rocket was the world's no. 1 tennis player as an amateur from 1961-1962 and as a pro from 1964-1970. He won the "Grand Slam" twice (all four majors in one year in 1962 and 1969) and eleven Grand Slam singles titles overall (despite not being allowed to play the Grand Slams for five years until the Open Era began in 1968). His 198 singles titles are the most in history.

Borg won head to head series 6-2

1978   Las Vegas WCT Indoor Carpet R16   Borg 64 62

1976   WITC SC, USA Outdoor Clay SF Borg 63 75

1976   Palm Springs CA Outdoor Hard QF Borg 62 67 76

1975   US Open Outdoor Clay R16 Borg 61 64 26 62

1975   WCT Finals Dallas Indoor Carpet SF   Borg   762 36 57 762 62

1974   Houston WCT   Outdoor Clay F Laver 765 62

1974   Tokyo WCT Outdoor Hard SF   Laver 63 75

1974   Barcelona WCT   Indoor Carpet R16   Borg 61 61

FACING
BJORN BORG

Bettina Bunge: We played mixed doubles together in Houston, Texas, in November of 1983 ($400,000 World Mixed Doubles Tournament at the 6,000 seat Astroarena). I could have slept with Borg back then, but I vehemently pushed his advances away. He was married.

(Note: Jimmy Connors and Chris Evert-Lloyd beat Roscoe Tanner and Andrea Jaeger in the final 64 62 64 for the $100,000 first prize.)

The German was a tennis professional from 1978-1989 and reached no. 6 in the world in 1983. In 1982 she was a Wimbledon semifinalist. Overall, Bunge won four career singles and four doubles titles.

Bjorn Borg and Leif Shiras

FACING
BJORN BORG

Larry Denyes: He lived with Bill Rompf for awhile in Bradenton. He would be a good one to talk to. Jose Lambert traveled to several tournaments with him as a coach/hitting partner. And of course, Nick. Borg was trying to make a comeback and was testing racquets while he was here. Maybe Ken Merritt would have dealt with him as a racquet technician. I just remember he was very accessible.

Imaged by Heritage Auctions, HA.com

LeRoy Neiman art work.

FACING
BJORN BORG

Joe Yanagisawa: I strung for Borg once at US Open. I was a racquet stringer at US Open first year at Flushing Meadows. He hated my string job [smiles]. He sent the racquet back to the stringing office manager to be restrung. Donnay wood racquet. eighty pounds VH Gut, seventeen gage. I guess I didn't get it exactly eighty pounds and he could feel it.

Alberto Ramirez Suarez art work.

FACING
BJORN BORG

Steve Carter: I hit with him and did some endorsements to help him make some money. IMG lost all his money. I know that while he was here in Bradenton, he was always leaving to go do an appearance here and there to have money to keep him going.

C2109EX
Nr. 1 Januar 197
DM 4.
ennis
magazin
ORT '78: Die großen Vier und ihre Verfolger
NISARM
sanfte
der
lung
RACKETS
Das Spiel mit
Spannung
und Gewicht
BESSER SPIELEN
So überwinden
Sie Ihr
Formtief
POSTER
BJÖRN
BORG

FACING
BJORN BORG

Gerard Faulkner: Forty years ago, the last of Bjorn Borg's eleventh slam titles and his sixth French Open title, was hoisted by this genius above his head at Roland Garros. Bjorn went on to make the finals of Wimbledon and the US Open also that year. I am an extremely avid fan of Bjorn's. I have collected years of statistics of Bjorn's career between 1974 and 1981 and have placed every statistic imaginable side by side with: Roy Emerson, Rod Laver, Jimmy Connors, John McEnroe, Peter Sampras, Andre Agassi, Ivan Lendl, Roger Federer, Rafael Nadal and Novak Djokovic, not surprisingly there are very few statistics where he is not the best or not in the top three amidst this stellar bunch of tennis royals.

He is the only six-plus slam champion who never lost in the first round in twenty-seven Grand Slam appearances.
How about, Bjorn winning a slam title with the least number of games won against him, losing only 32 games in the 1978 French Open victory.

He won his first fifty titles (must include multiple slams) at an earlier age and in less attempts than any other player in history.

No fellow slam winner that he played had a better overall head-to-head record against Borg. McEnroe and Borg tied at 7-7, is the closest he had in this regard. John Newcombe was 3-2 vs. a young Borg.

Borg beat Connors the last ten times they played on the Tour including the final meeting in 1981 US Open semifinal.

The number of Grand Slams it took to win eleven Grand Slam titles: Borg took 25, Laver 33, Sampras, 37, Federer, 33, Nadal 32 and Djokovic 45. To win fourteen slams it took Sampras 52, Federer 40, Nadal 38 and Djokovic 56.

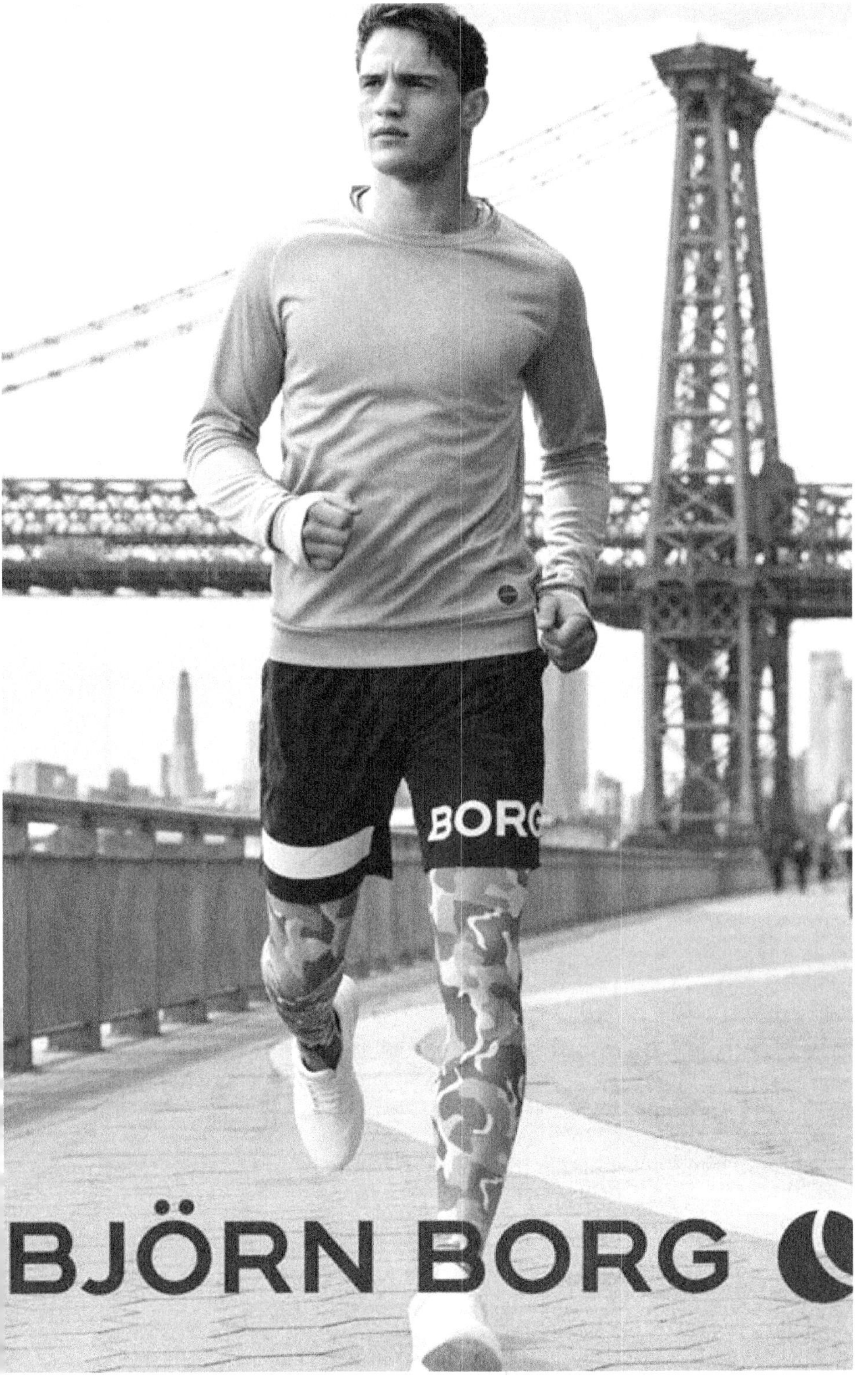
BORG
BJÖRN BORG

FACING
BJORN BORG

Anonymous: Borg was one of the driving reasons I loved tennis as a young man, and the enjoyment of the sport has grown through the years. I had the pleasure of meeting Bjorn several times, seeing him play live even more, and had the honor of hitting with him and Vitas back in the mid-80s after his retirement. First time I met him... party at Liza Minnelli's New York City apartment. His off-court demeanor was fun. Who knew? Liza was so excited to hold court, pun intended, with the great Borg and this was obvious as she was beaming all evening. No, Borg didn't sing that night [smiles].

Question: How did you know Liza Minelli?

Anonymous: I knew her since 1979 but was part of her inner circle from 1984-1990 due to a roommate being a personal assistant.

Question: How did you get to meet Borg and hit with him?

Anonymous: I'm friends with Liza Minnelli and played tennis with her husband Mark Gero in the mid-80s, and he was good pals with Vitas Gerulaitis. Mark and I went out to Vitas's place on Long Island and played doubles with he and Bjorn, who gave me his Donnay racquet. I still have it. I'm under a PDA with Liza, but one day may write my own book.

FACING
BJORN BORG

Howard Winitsky: A memorable match I played at Roland Garros... I recall being down two sets to love against Borg in the finals, and I came back to beat him 0, 0, 0 in the third, fourth, and fifth sets. And then the damn dog woke me up from my dream [smiles].

Bjorn Borg and Ron Koenig.

FACING
BJORN BORG

Bill Lloyd: Me and Kim Warwick went to a Rolling Stones concert with Bjorn and (future wife) Mariana, before the final of the French Open, in Paris 1978. What happened there will stay there!

FACING
BJORN BORG

John William Hayes: I played with Borg in a doubles exhibition in Greenwich, CT. We beat Rod Laver and Tim Norton. As a teenager I was the local yokel in the doubles portions of every exhibition that came to town - Laver twice, Borg, Roy Emerson, Arthur Ashe, Colin Dibley, Gene Scott and Clark Graebner. I don't have any memories from that exhibition playing with Borg. I did know Borg a little from the Tour, and always found him to be a very nice guy.

MENSUEL - N° 27 - JUIN 1978 - 9 F
Tennis
MAGAZINE
VILAS - BORG
LE
DUEL
SPECIAL
ROLAND-
GARROS

FACING
BJORN BORG

Jim Tarsy: Borg was my neighbor, he lived on the next street, Forest Drive, in Sands Point (Long Island, NY). Borg and I both belonged to the Port Washington Tennis Academy. He wasn't a member but he trained there for the US Open. I watched him. Wood racquet. He and his coach would call his racquet a 'shovel' in Swedish. How do I know this? I had a Swedish friend who listened to them in practice. He bought the house for $5m and then sold it two years later.

FACING
BJORN BORG

Swedish newspaper reporter: "That's why reporters are afraid of Bjorn. They don't want to lose a chance to talk to him. They don't like to be treated as an enemy. I know what that's like. I criticized him in the paper for not playing Davis Cup and he didn't want to talk to me again for years. I don't care much now but it hurt me in my job. He is our most famous athlete yet I couldn't get near him."

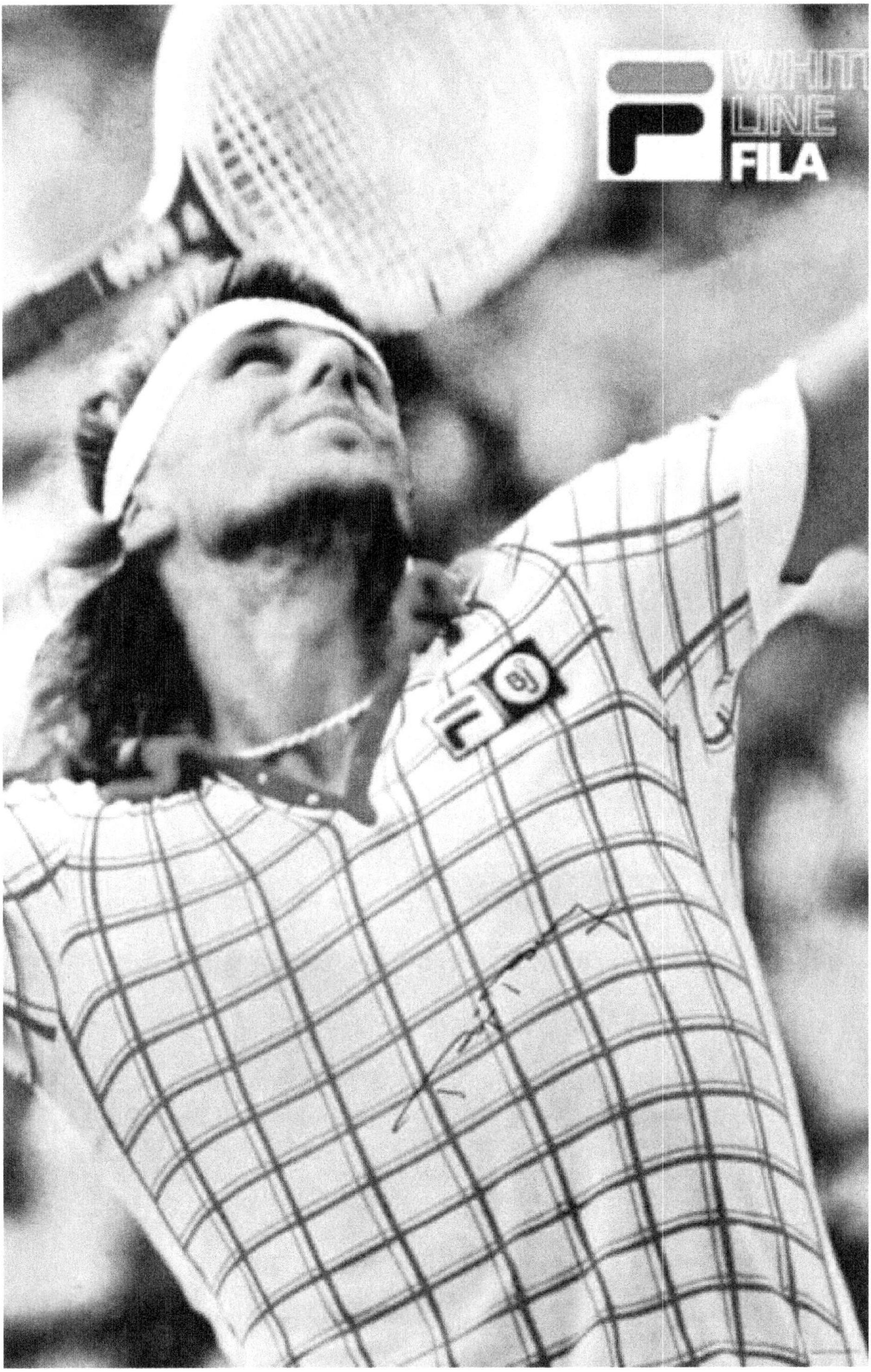
WHITE
LINE
FILA

FACING
BJORN BORG

Johan Kriek: 1980 US Open when I played Bjorn Borg in the semis, was leading two sets to love and then he woke up. I lost 4-6, 4-6, 6-1, 6-1, 6-1.

Question: You have beaten Borg (by walkover). How did you beat him?

Johan Kriek: With a frying pan... in my sleep [smiles].

Speedy and determined South African endured an 'against all odds' journey to a pro tennis career, which was sensationally highlighted by consecutive Australian Open conquests in 1981, 1982. Kriek collected 14 career singles titles total, the first in Sarasota, Florida in 1979, the final in Livingston, NJ in 1987.

Borg won head to head series 3-0

1980   US Open Outdoor Hard SF Borg 46 46 61 61 61

1979   WCT Challenge Cup Canada Indoor Carpet   RR   Borg 64 62

1979   Basel   Indoor Hard QF   Kriek W/O

1979   Rotterdam WCT Indoor Carpet QF Borg 64 62

FACING
BJORN BORG

Stefan Edberg: I had the opportunity to practice with Borg when I was fifteen or sixteen. One of the things I remember about that experience was Borg wanted to run to pick up balls so the practice would move more fluently [smiles].

Elegant and explosive, the swooping, striking, stoic Swede inflicted devastation on the ATP Tour from 1983 to 1996, collecting six Grand Slams in singles, two each in Melbourne, Wimbledon and New York. Seventeen-year-old Michael Chang thwarted Edberg in the 1989 Roland Garros final from a 2-1 set deficit.

FACING
BJORN BORG

John McEnroe: My best rival, my great friend Bjorn Borg. We first played in 1978 in Stockholm. He's very nice. He always gives me some free (Bjorn Borg brand) underwear when I come to Stockholm. I think he started a revolution in tennis (inspired the careers of Mats Wilander, Stefan Edberg, Anders Jarryd, Jonas Bjorkman, Thomas Enqvist, Magnus Larsson, etc). My most famous match was when I lost to him in the Wimbledon final in 1980, when I won the fourth set tiebreaker and he won the fifth set. Then I beat him the next year but nobody remembers [smiles]. I think he's the only one of my rivals who I always got along with, the rest of them I was always fighting with. Bjorn and I are similar, we have the same sense of humor, we think about things similarly. Bjorn is the only guy I never yelled at. He's the only guy I never had a problem with, on or off the court. One time I was going crazy. If you can believe that [smiles]. I was going crazy late in the match, it was 5-5 in the third set. And I could see Borg across the net pointing to me to come to net. I said (to myself),

Oh my God, he's going to tell me I'm the biggest asshole. He said, This is all right, this is good. We're both enjoying this. And at first I thought, Is he trying to play some kind of mind game? The great Bjorn Borg gave me some respect in this crazy moment. I thought, This is excellent. I felt like the luckiest guy in the world.

The mercurial rebel artist from New York passionately willed his way to the top, entertaining, awe-inspiring and amusing galleries who still vividly remember his masterpieces, melodramas and athletic magic. McEnroe won seven Grand Slam titles (four US Open, three Wimbledon), 77 singles titles and 77 doubles titles. He also won five Wimbledon doubles titles, four US Open doubles titles and the first in mixed doubles as a teenager at Roland Garros with Mary Carillo.

Head to head series tied 7-7

1981   US Open Outdoor Hard F McEnroe   46 62 64 63

1981   Wimbledon Outdoor Grass F McEnroe   46 76 76 64

1981   Milan WCT Indoor Carpet F McEnroe   76 64

1980   Masters NY Indoor Carpet RR Borg   64 67 76

1980   Stockholm Indoor Carpet F Bjorn Borg   63 64

1980   US Open Outdoor Hard F McEnroe 76 61 67 57 64

1980   Wimbledon Outdoor Grass F Borg 16 75 63 67 86

1979   Masters NY Indoor Carpet SF   Borg 67 63 76

1979 Toronto Outdoor Hard F Borg 63 63

1979 WCT Finals TX Indoor Carpet F McEnroe 75 46 62 76

1979 Rotterdam WCT Indoor Carpet F Borg 64 62

1979 New Orleans WCT Indoor Carpet SF McEnroe 57 61 76

1979 Richmond WCT Indoor Carpet SF Borg 46 76 63

1978 Stockholm Indoor Hard SF McEnroe 63 64

FACING
BJORN BORG

Steve Siebold: I hit with him in an exhibition in Chicago in 1976 with Rod Laver. Two great guys.

FACING
BJORN BORG

Harold Solomon: Let me tell you about how good Bjorn Borg was. In 1980 I was playing really well and two weeks before the French Open I had just beaten Guillermo Vilas in five sets in the finals of the German Open. Bjorn and I had arranged to practice the last week before the French at the Pigeon Club in Paris. We started Tuesday and played three out of five sets every day. He beat me in three straight sets every day and I think I only got to 6-3 once in the four days snd we would play for three to four hours each time, but he would never get tired and his ball was so heavy it would bounce high and push your racquet back. It was very hard to penetrate off his ball, I had to jump off the ground on almost every ball. Anyway, after he kills me again Friday he says to me: "Same time tomorrow?" And I said: "Are you out of your mind?! Four days in a row and I haven't won a set!" And he just smiles! Of course we play in the semifinals and he beats me like a drum (62 62 60), four days of practice and one semi-finals and not one set for me. I have so many Borg stories. Needless to say until Nadal came along I thought he was by far the best ever on clay and a really good guy totally unaffected by who he was, and he was the closest tennis player to ever be like a rock star. We would do exhibition tours in Europe and you have never seen girls and women of all ages go totally out of their minds for him!

Called "The Human Backboard" for his extraordinary defensive and counterpunching skills, the gritty American won 22 singles titles, earned a no. 5 world ranking in 1980 and contested the 1976 Roland Garros final which he lost in four sets to Panatta. Solomon's tenacity, concentration and "moonballs" also earned nine Davis Cup singles victories for USA.

Borg won head to head series 15-0

1980   Roland Garros Outdoor Clay SF Borg 62 62 60

1980   Las Vegas Outdoor Hard F Borg 63 61

1978   WCT Challenge Cup Jamaica Outdoor Hard RR Borg 63 62

1978   Tokyo Indoor Carpet QF   Borg 61 62

1978   US Open Outdoor Hard R16   Borg 62 62 60

1978   Rome Italy Outdoor Clay QF Borg   62 61

1978   Richmond WCT   Indoor Carpet R16 Borg 63 62

1978   Birmingham WCT Indoor Carpet R32 Borg 62 64

1976   Boston Outdoor Clay F   Borg 67 64 61 62

1976   WCT Finals Indoor Carpet SF Borg 75 60 63

1975   Masters Sweden Indoor Carpet RR Borg 62 62

1975   Roland Garros Outdoor Clay QF Borg 61 75 64

1974   Roland Garros Outdoor Clay   SF Borg 64 26 62 61

1974   Houston WCT Outdoor Clay R16 Borg 63 64

1974   Tokyo WCT Outdoor Hard R32 Borg 16 62 60

FACING
BJORN BORG

Donald Dell: Bjorn Borg was known for having ice water in his veins. His nickname was "The Iceman." The greater the pressure, the better he seemed to play. We never represented Borg (as an agent/manager) but I once asked him how he managed to remain so cool under pressure. I remember what he said: "Actually I get terrified. If it's my serve, sometimes I think I'm not even going to be able to toss the ball up in the air. My senses are so on edge I can hear someone in the stands coughing in the top row. But I know that if I can just put the ball in play, my strokes are going to take over and I'll be fine."

The Yale Grad is an American sports attorney, writer, television commentator, and former tennis player. The first sports agent in professional tennis represented Arthur Ashe, Stan Smith, Jimmy Connors, and Ivan Lendl during the "golden age" of pro tennis (1975 to 1985). In 1970 Dell founded Professional Services (ProServ), one of the nation's first sports marketing firms.

FACING
BJORN BORG

Lisa Bonder-Kerkorian: I traveled with him during an exhibition tour in Japan way back in the 80's. Wow. They loved him there. He was like a God to them. He was definitely quiet. A humble guy. He took all the adoration and adulation in stride. Always kind. Super generous with signing autographs and seemed to really appreciate his fans.

The former WTA pro (1981-1991) from Columbus, Ohio won four singles titles and achieved a world ranking of no. 9 in 1984.

FACING
BJORN BORG

Gene Mayer: Borg was willing to stay the night if he felt he needed to. His strokes were not truly phenomenal, other players hit the ball better. Patience, stamina and savvy made him the great player he was. I beat him at Masters at Madison Square Garden in 1980 for the first time 6-0 6-3. My wife said I didn't miss a shot for the first four games.

Question: What is your first memory of Bjorn Borg?

Gene Mayer: My first memory of Borg is what most people thought - the external, the long, flowing blonde hair, the headband, the Swedish mystique. He was a good guy once you got to know him, but you didn't get to know him right away. The quietness of his persona enhanced the mystique.

Question: You gave Borg a bagel in a match at the January 1981 Masters at Madison Square Garden. Your memories of this match?

Gene Mayer: When people ask me what is the best tennis you ever played I generally answer a time I played on some backyard court in a practice match that nobody saw. When I played Borg at the Masters the ATP season was a different time frame. Back then, the Masters started the season in January. Everybody was getting into it after a break in December. In my first match that year at Masters I beat John McEnroe in three sets in a rowdy atmosphere in Madison Square Garden (36 76 62). Then I beat Jose Luis Clerc (63 75). After that match I was really sore. I remember the next day I was so sore that I was asking for help, what can I do? Someone said to get on the stationary bike. So before the match with Borg I did about thirty minutes on the bike. I was sweating profusely. I was cooked. And then we went out and played and I think I won the first nine games. Maybe it was a good way to warm up. That was maybe the best segment of tennis I ever played - that half hour against Borg.

Question: Do you remember your tactics in that win vs Borg which was your first and only career win vs. Borg in ATP after seven losses.

Gene Mayer: By that point, I was starting to understand how to play Bjorn. I played him three times earlier in 1980, at Nations Cup in German, Wimbledon and Stockholm. He was very different in that time period, how he played. Most people would try take over the point against him, take position on the court. He was a reactive player. I had to almost under-play to start the point. Not give him pace. Give him off pace, to start, high, loopy balls. Then when you got the chance with the right ball, you attack, attack well and quickly. It was a combination of I played well and tactically smart, get the right ball and hurt him effectively. We played on an indoor court which was to my advantage. It was so much harder to hurt him on clay. I played him one time on clay at Nations Cup, he won 63 75.

Question: Do you have any standout memories of Borg on or off court?

Gene Mayer: I can remember sitting with Borg and we were in Denver (1977). It was the first time we played in the ATP. We were about to go on and play. They had to clear the arena due to some kind of power issue. They said we had time to go back to the hotel. But we sat and talked instead of going back to the hotel. In our conversation we shared almost identical stories. Guys are generally boisterous on the court but you're stoic... he said, Let me tell you a story... When I was fourteen I went nuts on the court, breaking racquets in a match. My father wouldn't let me play tennis for six weeks. He put my racquets in a kitchen closet. I saw my racquets but I couldn't play. I learned a lesson.

And then I told a similar story... At 13 I lost to kid in my age group and I threw my racquet and behaved badly. And my father told me, Next time that happens you won't play again. He didn't let me play for two months. So we had almost identical stories. It was a reminder to us - there's a way conduct yourself on the court and a way not to. It was an important lesson from our parents early on in our tennis careers.

Then we played the match in Denver and he won 64 63.

Question: Any other memorable matches with Borg?

Gene Mayer: Playing him at Wimbledon (1980) in quarterfinals. That was a standout because it was on center court, against Bjorn Borg, obviously he was racking up the Wimbledon titles. I had opportunities galore in that match (lost 57 36 57). I was up. It was a sort of constant reminder - he didn't necessarily beat you with impressive shots. When it came down to it, he missed less balls, he ran better and he competed better. I played well but in the key points he out-competed me in that match.

Question: Last time you actually saw Borg?

Gene Mayer: We were seeing each other all the time for the Jimmy Connors senior tour. The last time was either at a senior Wimbledon event which they don't have any more, or at the French Open that he was popping in to award the trophy. It's been a while, up until the last five or eight years. Bjorn still looks the same, as fit as ever. Here's a funny memory. Playing in a senior event on an island, Baltic Aland in the summer. It was an eight-man event. Even in Sweden he is a huge deal. One night we did an appearance. I had my son with me. At the hotel. The hotel had an entertainment area, casino, and ballroom for dinner. I remember walking with Bjorn, it's maybe 9 pm, walking through this long hallway, we were walking and seeing and stepping over bodies on the ground. I said, What is going on here? Bjorn said, This is Scandinavian summer. Some people drink a lot, some people drink too much [laughs]. Okay.

Then we sat at a formed table, with people sitting around the table for dinner. Every seat had a fifth of vodka. At our table, looking across at a guy - my son is with me, he was 12 then - the guy is about two-thirds done with his bottle of vodka and he's no slumped over, his face in his dessert. Then he lifted his head and next thing is he's having another drink. They have a different outlook towards alcohol consumption I'd never seen before. Which is not that uncommon in Scandinavian countries.

The double-fisted player who grew up in the New York City suburb of Packanack Lake, NJ, ascended to no. 4 in the world, won 14 singles, 15 doubles titles and the 1979 Roland Garros doubles crown with older brother Sandy.

Borg won head to head series 7-1

1980   Masters NY Indoor Carpet RR Mayer 60 63

1980   Stockholm Indoor Carpet   SF   Borg 62 75

1980   Wimbledon Outdoor Grass QF Borg 75 63 75

1980   Nations Cup Germany Outdoor Clay RR Borg 63 75

1979   Toronto Outdoor Hard QF   Borg 64 61

1979   Las Vegas Outdoor Hard SF Borg 61 61

1979   New Orleans WCT Indoor Carpet R32   Borg 64 63

1977   Denver Indoor Carpet   R32   Borg 64 63

FACING
BJORN BORG

Mats Torngren: The morning after the epic 1977 Wimbledon semifinal (64 36 63 36 86) Vitas Gerulaitis and Björn took a practice session at 10 am. Borg and Bergelin were greatly impressed by this and Björn and Vitas had a great workout. And the rest is history... Borg won the final against Connors in five sets. From that day on they were best friends. Notably, Vitas never won a competive match against Björn (17-0 in Borg's favor).

FACING
BJORN BORG

Erik Siklos: I was there at Borg's comeback tournament in Monte Carlo in 1991 when he played Jordi Arrese in the first round and lost 62 63 inside a packed stadium. He played with an old, small, outdated wooden racquet and lost in about seventy-five minutes. What I also remember is he didn't use the official car (Volvo) of the tournament … he arrived with a classic VW Beetle. I saw him getting into the car at the front of the hotel [smiles].

FACING
BJORN BORG

Ernesto Ruiz-Bry: When I was coaching Guillermo Vilas, he told me a story he played nineteen practice sets in one day with Borg. They were training together on an island in the Caribbean.

FACING
BJORN BORG

Nicolai Herlofson: What an enigmatic person he was. I can't say it was an encounter, but I met him when I was twelve and he played his last Monte Carlo 1982 - counting out the embarrassing comeback. Got his autograph and thought I had met God. Bjorn lost to Yannick Noah. Have you seen footage of him from 1982? He seemed deeply depressed. I am always happy to see him now on TV. Glad he made it through.

FACING
BJORN BORG

Jimmy Connors: The matches Borg and I play are going to be around a lot longer than we are. Maybe when we're seventy or so, people will still be talking about them. I don't want them to talk about this one particularly (1978 Wimbledon final loss to Borg 62 62 63), but there'll be plenty more. The season is young.

An Australian writer asked if Connors would play the Australian Open if Borg won the US Open and had a chance to win the Grand Slam. "I may follow him to the ends of the earth now," replied Connors.

One of the purest warriors in the history of sport, "Jimbo" symbolized a nation, a generation. His 1991 US Open heroics undoubtedly spawned and inspired countless other future champions.

Borg won head to head series 15-8

1981   US Open Outdoor Hard SF   Borg 62 75 64

1981   Wimbledon Outdoor Grass SF   Borg 06 46 63 60 64

1980   Masters NY Indoor Carpet SF Borg 64 67 63

1980   Salisbury WCT Indoor Carpet RR Borg 63 61

1979   Masters NY Indoor Carpet RR Borg 36 63 76

1979   WCT Challenge Cup Canada Indoor Carpet F Borg 64 62 26 64

1979   Tokyo   Indoor Carpet F   Borg   62 62

1979   Wimbledon Outdoor Grass SF   Borg 62 63 62

1979   Las Vegas   Outdoor Hard   F Borg 63 62

1979   Pepsi Grand Slam FL   Outdoor Clay F Borg 62 63

1978   US Open Outdoor Hard F   Connors 64 62 62

1978   Wimbledon   Outdoor Grass   F Borg 62 62 63

1978   Pepsi Grand Slam FL Outdoor Clay F Borg 76 36 61

1977   Masters NY Indoor Carpet F Connors 64 16 64

1977   Wimbledon Outdoor Grass F Borg 36 62 61 57 64

1977   Pepsi Grand Slam FL   Outdoor Clay F Borg 64 57 63

1976   US Open Outdoor Clay F Connors 64 36 76 64

1976   Palm Springs CA Outdoor Hard SF   Connors 64 61

1976   Philadelphia WCT Indoor Carpet F Connors 765 64 60

1975   Stockholm   Indoor Hard SF Connors 62 76

1975   US Open Outdoor Clay SF Connors 75 75 75

1974   Indianapolis   Outdoor Clay F Connors 57 63 64

1973   Stockholm   Indoor Hard   SF Borg 64 36 76

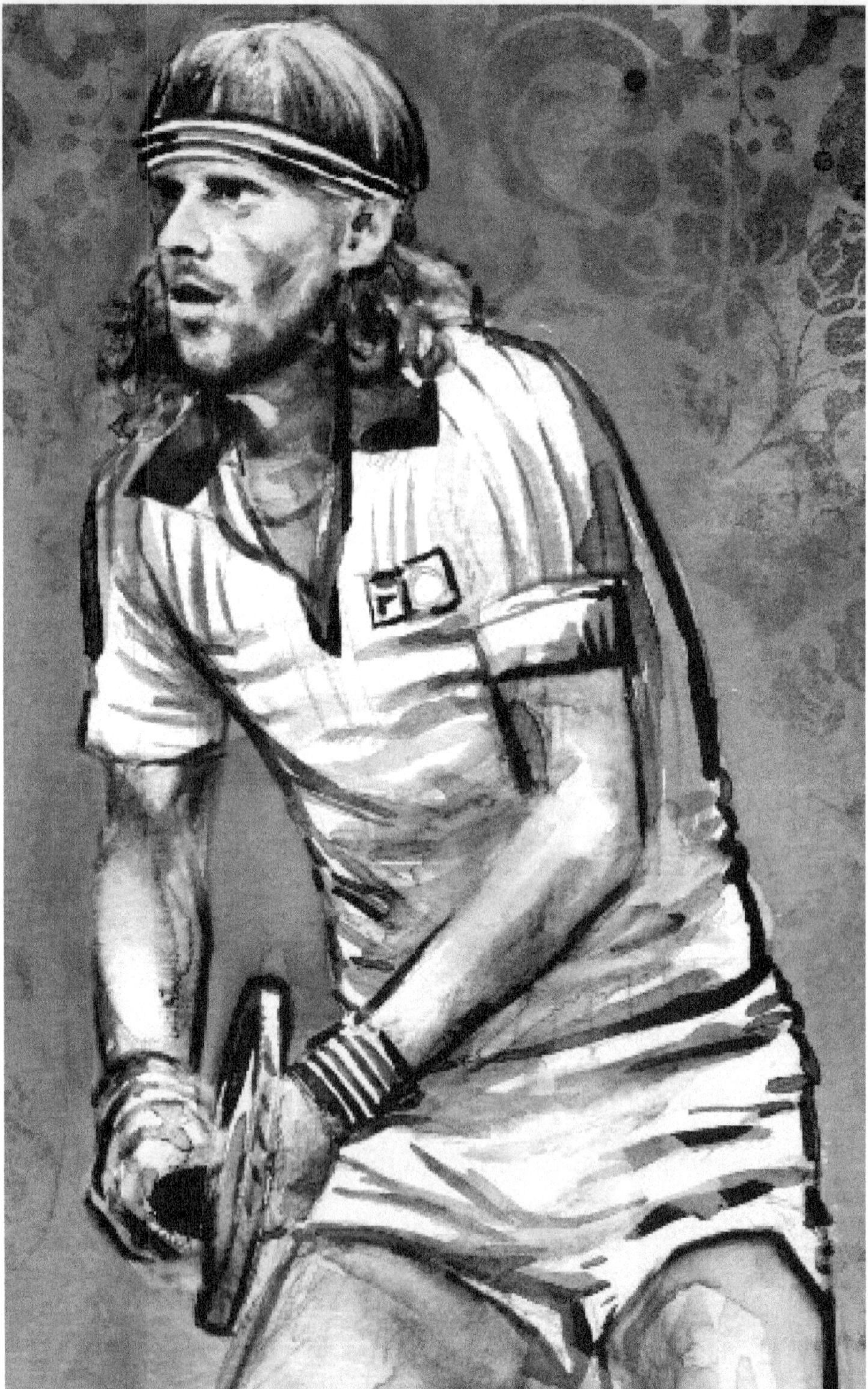

FILA

FACING
BJORN BORG

Guillermo Vilas: It's not that difficult to figure out. We're going to play tennis. Each of us will have a racquet and one of us will win. We play the same game. We hit topspin and we know what the other does best… He played so well, he didn't give me any chances at all. I knew if I was going to play from the baseline all the time, I was going to win more games but not the match. So I tried different tactics, but it did not work. Nothing worked.

The introspective Young Bull of the Pampas attracted worldwide legions of supporters, as symbolized when he was carried off the Forest Hills court by loving New Yorkers who so admired his examples of sportsmanship, determination and commitment to excellence.

Borg won head to head series 17-5

1980   Nations Cup Germany   Outdoor Clay   SF Vilas 63 16 61
1980   Monte Carlo WCT Outdoor Clay   F Borg   61 60 62

1980	Pepsi Grand Slam FL	Outdoor Clay	SF	Borg	62 63
1979	Pepsi Grand Slam FL	Outdoor Clay	SF	Borg	63 63
1979	Richmond WCT	Indoor Carpet	F	Borg	63 61
1978	Roland Garros	Outdoor Clay	F	Borg	61 61 63
1977	Masters NY	Indoor Carpet	SF	Borg	63 63
1977	Monte Carlo WCT	Outdoor Clay	SF	Borg	62 63
1977	Nice	Outdoor Clay	F	Borg	64 16 62 60
1976	Wimbledon	Outdoor Grass	QF	Borg	63 60 62
1976	WCT Finals TX	Indoor Carpet	F	Borg	16 61 75 61
1976	Sao Paulo WCT	Indoor Carpet	F	Borg	764 62
1975	Masters Sweden	Indoor Carpet	RR	Vilas	75 46 61
1975	Barcelona	Outdoor Clay	SF	Borg	63 61 76
1975	Boston	Outdoor Clay	F	Borg	63 64 62
1975	Roland Garros	Outdoor Clay	F	Borg	62 63 64
1974	Masters Australia	Outdoor Grass	RR	Vilas	75 61
1974	Toronto	Outdoor Clay	QF	Vilas	76 60
1974	Rome	Outdoor Clay	SF	Borg	26 36 63 64 75
1974	Houston WCT	Outdoor Clay	QF	Borg	62 64
1974	Tokyo WCT	Outdoor Hard	QF	Borg	64 63
1973	Buenos Aires	Outdoor Clay	F	Vilas	36 67 64 66 RET

Bjorn Borg and Juan Coronel.

FACING
BJORN BORG

John Lloyd: Although I, of course, lost to Borg many times I did beat him once at Monte Carlo in the quarterfinal of a WCT event. Now before you pass out in disbelief, rumors were that he was out until 4 am the night before with a few ladies. Of course when I brag about the result I forget to mention that fact. Just between you and me [smiles].

Dynamic, dashing and debonair, the Hollywood handsome Brit achieved his greatest results in mixed doubles, winning three Grand Slam titles with Australian Wendy Turnbull in the early 1980s. His lone ATP singles championship was earned at Merion in 1974.

Borg won head to head series 5-1

1977   Wembley Indoor Carpet F   Borg 64 64 63

1977   Basel Indoor Hard F   Borg 64 62 63

1977   Memphis Indoor Carpet R16 Borg 06 62 64

1976　Stockholm Indoor Hard　R16　Borg　62 67 76

1976　US Open　Outdoor Clay　R32　Borg　63 63

1975　Monte Carlo WCT　Outdoor Clay　QF　Lloyd　60 57 64

FACING
BJORN BORG

Steve Krulevitz: Practicing with Bjorn on clay was like running up a hill. I hit with him the second week of the French in 1980 and before his semi we played two sets. After he showered and went to Roland Garros for his match (defeated Harold Solomon 62 62 60). I went back to the hotel and took a nap. It was a great week hanging with Bjorn and coach Lennart Bergelin. We had a lot of laughs.

American Krulevitz turned pro in 1973 and recorded an ATP singles record of 121-202. His highest ATP singles ranking was no. 70 in 1981. In doubles he won four ATP titles.

FACING
BJORN BORG

Stan Smith: I think there are six that are the best in history. Sampras, Laver, Borg and the Big Three: Federer, Nadal and Djokovic. Fortunately, these three continue to play. Tennis fans around the world had the opportunity to see three of the best at the same time. It is a special era, which will end in a few years. I think the only one who would have had great achievements in the past era is Roger Federer, because he has a very fair, precise style of play. In fact, for many years he played with a small hoop racquet. One of the questions I ask myself about Laver, who played seventeen Grand Slam finals and won eleven, and who did not play the majors for almost six years... is how many more he could have had? He could well have won ten more titles in those twenty-four tournaments that he did not play, because he dominated before and after.

A world no. 1 tennis player and two-time Grand Slam singles champion at US Open in 1971 and Wimbledon in 1972, Smith also teamed with Bob

Lutz as one of the most successful doubles teams of all time. The adidas white tennis shoe renamed the "Stan Smith" in 1978. It's estimated over 25,000,000 pairs of the iconic shoes have been sold.

Borg won head head to head series 5-2

1981   Milan WCT Indoor Carpet   QF   Borg   60 62

1978   Milan WCT Indoor Carpet   SF   Borg   67 60 62

1976   Palm Springs Outdoor Hard R16 Borg   76 75

1976   Memphis WCT Indoor Carpet   SF   Smith   761 63

1975   Roland Garros Outdoor Clay R16 Borg   62 63 60

1974   WITC SC Outdoor Carpet   SF   Borg   26 64 60

1973   Bastad Outdoor Clay   SF   Smith   64 64 62

FACING
BJORN BORG

Mohammad Ali Akbar: Practiced with him 1987. He had started to hit with minimum topspin. Said it took too much energy. He had total focus on the ball, all the time. Feet never stopped moving. A big callus in the middle of his right hand. He felt it wasn't the surface of the court but the type of ball that made the most difference for him. His eyes were always very focused on the ball. Even when he came to the net to pick up a ball lying on the ground his focus would be only on the ball. A lesson, perhaps!

FACING
BJORN BORG

David Bush: I was lucky enough to hit with him when he was retired, for a few years and we did play exhibition doubles against each other in Phuket, Thailand. Even then his feet were like hovercrafts, effortlessly floating/moving around the court. Awesome guy and was very kind to me on court! As well as great fun off court. Physically he was still a freak, in great shape and basically, kept me on a string, just moved me around till he chose to pull the trigger on a shot. In a practice set, apparently I was up 40-0, 40-15 in four games...got two of them in a set! He was not hugely overpowering, he just owned the court and position on it. Did beat him in the doubles - but think his partner hit 90% of the shots!

FACING
BJORN BORG

Lennart Bergelin (Borg's coach): Bjorn was always difficult to beat over five sets for two reasons. One, he was physically stronger than most players. Second, I have seldom come across anyone who so hated to lose, even in a practice match.

FACING
BJORN BORG

Mariana Simonescu (Borg's former wife): I played a lot with Lennart. And we also fight against each other. When we play, we like to beat each other so much. Sometimes we play points with Bjorn. Bjorn always makes fun of us, because he beat us so badly.

Question: Does he never let you win?

Mariana Simonescu: Never. He never let anyone win [smiles].

FACING
BJORN BORG

Rayni Fox Borinsky: I only met him once when we were juniors when he played the Orange Bowl. I only remember being at a house - everyone was housed back then. He was playing ping pong but other players were there and I had a crush on Corrado Barazzutti if I recall, so my attentions were going in that direction! Flamingo Park was a great site, the tournament was awesome.

FACING
BJORN BORG

Corrado Barazzutti: Bjorn Borg was the toughest competitor I ever encountered, for sure. It was very tough to beat him. Impossible for me [laughs]. We played a lot of times but I never win.

The clever Italian won five ATP singles titles and achieved an overall record of 317-231. His best ranking was no. 7 in the world.

Borg won head to head series 10-0

1980   Roland Garros Outdoor Clay QF   Borg   60 63 63

1979   Palermo   Outdoor Clay F   Borg   64 60 64

1978   Bastad Outdoor Clay F   Borg   61 62

1978   Roland Garros Outdoor Clay SF   Borg   60 61 60

1977   Monte Carlo Outdoor Clay F   Borg   63 75 60

1975   Barcelona Indoor Carpet R32   Borg   63 36 63

1974   Bastad Outdoor Clay QF   Borg   64 36 62

1973   Monte Carlo Outdoor Clay R16   Borg   62 63

1973   Barcelona Outdoor Clay R32   Borg   16 64 62

1973   Valencia Outdoor Clay R32   Borg   64 62

FACING
BJORN BORG

Marcos Manqueros: I played against him in an exhibition doubles in Hong Kong during his Seniors tour. Although I don't remember him as blinding fast, what I do remember is that even in casual games, his eyes were as focused as a hawk on every ball, even the easy ones.

FACING
BJORN BORG

Andrei Cherkasov: I played doubles with Bjorn in Moscow 1993. Never forget how spectators cheered for him against (Alexander) Volkov (in singles) in Russia! Incredible! (Volkov, then ranked 17 in the world, won 46 63 76 (9-7).)

Question: Did you win in doubles with Borg? Against who?

Andrei Cherkasov: We lost first round (to Jared Palmer and Bent-Ove Pedersen 6-2 6-2). But he's a great person and player.

Question: Did Borg ask you to play doubles?

Andrei Cherkasov: No, we had the same agent.

Andrei Cherkasov won the first two Kremlin Cup singles titles in Moscow and reached no. 13 in the world. He also defeated Pete Sampras at the 1992 Barcelona Olympics from two sets down.

FACING
BJORN BORG

Emilio Benfele Alvarez: The only time I saw him play, actually was his first comeback, in Zaragoza, Spain in a brand new ATP tournament...he was playing indoors against Omar Camporese. You could cut the air with a knife from everyone's expectation and excitement.

The Spaniard won 45 ATP singles matches and his best singles ranking was 81.

FACING
BJORN BORG

Jorge Andrew: The first time I played Bjorn was in Wimbledon 1975 first round, I qualified, he just won the Italian and French Open at seventeen years old. I lost in three straight sets, don't remember the score, or don't want to remember it. He was one of the fastest players I ever played. The second time we played was in an exhibition at my club in the Altamira Tennis Club in Caracas, Venezuela, he won 9-7; I had one set point on his serve at 6-7 30-40, came to the net with a very good approach shot, he hit one of his traditional backhands passing shots cross court. After that I never had a chance.

The Caracas, Venezuela born Andrew was 37-114 in his ATP career and his top ranking in singles was 66.

Borg won head to head series 1-0
1975 Wimbledon Outdoor grass   R128   Borg   62 64 64

FACING
BJORN BORG

Henner Lenhardt: I was fortunate enough to meet a member of the Monte Carlo Country Club who asked me to be his personal pro in the summers and so was able to spend a month at the club for five years. In 1991 Borg was attempting a comeback and somehow I got a chance to practice with him. I was very excited and nervous at the same time. I don't think I missed a ball the first 30 minutes. He wanted to play some games and he said he normally switches sides every three games. The first couple games were close and then I was absolutely spent. I was physically exhausted and emotionally drained with the excitement. He was very gracious and it is one of my favorite memories playing tennis.

FACING
BJORN BORG

Tim Taylor: I last played Bjorn ten years ago in a seniors tournament which I edged in two tiebreaks, I stayed away from his backhand which he could still thread through the eye of a needle.

Bjorn Borg with Tim Taylor.

FACING
BJORN BORG

Michel Loutchaninoff: I worked some of his matches as a ballboy and later hit with him at one of his clinics he did in the late '70s with Vitas... but he was so private. Once he finished at the US Open, he would bolt. Stayed in a tight cocoon - was always nice but once he was done he was gone.

First he was super nice and only wanted to deal with the kids and us. He was like a rock star and press were all over the place. He really had no privacy - also never alone. Always had Lennart or his girlfriend at the hip.

He spoke French and since I did as well he was always cool talking to me in French and discussing the Racing Club in Paris that he liked.

But he was very cool and liked to talk about football - Swedish national team - and Swedish hockey - I'm a huge Montreal Canadian fan - and he loves to rave about them and Guy Lafleur, etc. He said he was upset he couldn't go see a game when in New York City as he would get mobbed. He told funny stories of sneaking into the Garden to catch a Ranger game once before The Masters in Madison Square Garden.

He did mention how playing at the US Open National Tennis Center was so hard due to the noise - the courts - the lights - and the smell of burning hamburgers when on court. Said it was a crazy place to play.

But he was really cool around Vitas as Vitas was always joking and messing with the kids. Borg would be so much looser around Vitas.

FACING
BJORN BORG

Liz Kennedy: I got to hit with Bjorn for a few minutes in Central Park (New York City) in 1979. I don't know how I was able to stand up! It was at a kid's clinic where you could hit with some of the pros. Guillermo Vilas and Vitas Gerulaitis were also there.

FACING
BJORN BORG

Gilad Bloom: I played him in doubles, when he made his "comeback" in 1993, it was in Washington DC. I played with Amos Mansdorf, his partner was Niklas Kroon. It was sad, full stadium, night match, but Borg didn't hold serve and we won 6-2 6-1. He didn't care.

Fast forward to 2011, WTT at John McEnroe Tennis Academy in New York City, Connors was scheduled to play Mac but got hurt a few days before the match, they already sold out the place so they had to get a big name. So Mac called his buddy Borg who was on vacation...Borg showed up the day before the match, I was Director of Tennis at McEnroe and as such had brought my (now ex) wife to watch the two legends. We had great seats and as I was about to eat my dinner and watch some tennis I got a call from my boss Johnny Mac who said to me: 'Bloomie, Borg is rusty, you need to go warm him up so he puts up a good show.'

I put the fork down and rushed to the court to warm up the legend - with my ex almost fainting when he came into the court and took a photo with him.

We played for forty-five minutes almost no misses, great rallies, at one point Bjorn said: Let's play a set, I was up 4-2 and 40-15 when the lady came to call him to the court and Borg went straight from the practice court to the stadium.

Borg played extremely well in the WTT match, it was 4-4 and in the 9-point tiebreaker Borg was up 4-2! I told my ex: "Watch how Borg is going to miss three shots in a row."

And he did - on purpose, blatantly... It was in the contract that he can't beat Mac in New York City. Borg was better than Mac that night.

Gilad Bloom, the left-hander from Israel, was once no. 61 in the world in singles and 62 in doubles. He won four ATP doubles titles - Seoul, Umag, Tel Aviv and Sao Paulo - but none in singles in three finals attempts.

FACING
BJORN BORG

Phil Secada: Back in my day during the very early 1970s, Bjorn Borg once hit against the wall at Hialeah's Milander Tennis Center, the same wall I hit on when I got started. He was only sixteen years old, getting ready to play the Orange Bowl. One of the adults there at the tennis courts, Dave Waters, said "Who is this guy?" None of us back then thought he would have been great. Certainly not a winner of five Wimbledon and six French Open titles!

FACING
BJORN BORG

Bunner Smith: He was in and out of Nick Bollettieri Tennis Academy quite often, mostly after his days playing at the top level. He was there during his comeback. It was a great place to train /practice with other great players. I only saw him in town a few times ..mostly during my hiatus from teaching 1992-2007, while I was the Jeep/Chrysler manager at Firkins Chrysler Jeep in Bradenton. Nick still drives Jeeps as do many of the old pros.

FACING
BJORN BORG

Arthur Ashe: He was bigger than the game. He was like Elvis or Liz Taylor or somebody.

FACING
BJORN BORG

Ilie Nastase: We're playing tennis. But Bjorn...he's playing something else.

FACING
BJORN BORG

Reno Manne: Way back in 1992, October or November, Borg came in to train at Nick Bollettieri Tennis Academy. He was 35. I was 22. His idea was to come in to NBTA to train to make some kind of comeback. Jose Lambert was to be his coach. We had the meeting on a Friday. He'd come on Monday. Gabe Jaramillo said I was to be his hitting partner. The Monday Borg came in I remember really well. I was extremely hungover. He came in early. I was sent to the indoor court to hit with him. So we get to the indoor court. He had his Donnay bag and NBTA shirt. He opens up his bag - by 1992 everyone was using graphite racquets - so he pulls out five wooden Donnay Borg Pro racquets. The same five he used when he last played Wimbledon in 1981. I just looked at him. He was an introvert. Didn't get much out of him. There was always a short pause before he said something. He hadn't played for years. To see him not be able to hit a ball was strange. His timing was off. He couldn't hit. He said he hadn't hit for years. Jose Lambert asked me why is he using wood racquets? I said I didn't get an answer, he doesn't like to talk much.

Eventually they managed to get a graphite into his hands. Those five Donnay wood racquets were actually the ones he played with at Wimbledon. He never got them restrung. He later gave me one of those racquets. I was his designated hitting partner to get him back in shape for some kind of comeback. I was also his personal chaffeur. Midway through the day one day I got a phone call. Back then there were no cell phones. He called the front desk of NBTA from a British pub. The guy said to come and pick him up, he's been here every night drinking. I got there. Where is he? It was a restaurant bar, separated by a screen. He's behind that screen. The guy said he comes here every night. He's on his ninth pint. Sitting by himself. Because he never talked to anyone. He had enough. Time to go. He was drunk. He got into the Mitsubishi van, we drove back to the academy. You could imagine the shape he was in after nine pints. He was in pretty good shape, he didn't have a belly. So that was the second shock. After seeing he was still using the wood racquets.

By the second week he started to talk. His drinking continued but every day on the court he was fresh as a daisy. I was told not to say anything. It was interesting. I was 22. He said he suffered depression, he was on drugs, he was trying to get his life together. I trained with him to get ready for exhibitions. Some years later - I hadn't seen him for years - I was in Oslo, Norway teaching tennis. He had started Borg clothing. I was invited to a party at Rockefellers's night club in Oslo. I went. I had no idea he would show up. I went to the restroom. Next to me I look and there's Borg taking a whiz. So he looks over, big smile. He recognized me. So we're both holding our dicks. It was a great night. We both got hammered. He was really nice to me that night, like I was a long lost brother. I'm friends with his wife on Facebook. He's not on Facebook but sometimes he communicates with me through her, he says hello, that's about it.

When the exhibitions started in late 1992 he was rusty. You know as a player if you don't play for a while you lose the timing. Three weeks of training wasn't enough. After three weeks hitting even then he wasn't very good. He couldn't serve at all. He really struggled with his serve timing.. He didn't take to the graphite racquets at all. Physically he looked good, he did some weights but I don't think he was in very good cardiovascular shape. In the beginning he got whooped. He was there because people just wanted to see him. He was playing some of the guys he used to play on the tour, so they kept it close for entertainment value.

To be so close to a legend of the sport - I was hitting with Agassi and Courier back then - I didn't appreciate it then as much as I do now. Now as I look back I was very blessed to have had that wonderful opportunity.

After the three weeks, he went on the road. He trained with Jose

Lambert. After each week he got more competitive. I remember saying to him you should stay for three months or six months to get in really good shape. But it was about money, he needed the income. He had the

FACING
BJORN BORG

Juan Coronel: I met Borg when I was coaching Gianni Ocleppo from Italy. We used to spend time in Monte Carlo and Borg lived there. Borg was a good friend of Vitas Gerulaitis and Vitas's buddy Tony Graham (who played at UCLA and was head pro at the Playboy Mansion). Borg was very easy going and one of the greatest of all time. In practice he was very intense, very focused on his movements and consistency of shots. I don't think we'll ever see someone winning Wimbledon five years in a row.

assing SH

GIONAL TENNIS & FITNESS MAGAZINE

VOLUME 1,
JULY/AUGUS

IN YOUR BACKYARD
Pro Tourneys Flock to the Tri-State Region

A&P Classic • Citibank Champions • GHI Bronx Classic • Waldbaum's Haml

---

There is no joy but calm. - **Alfred, Lord Tennyson**

Defense always beats attack - if the defense is good enough. - **Former Heavyweight Champion Jack Johnson**

No two men can be half an hour together, but one shall acquire an evident superiority over the other. - **Samuel Johnson**

In my walks, every man I meet is my superior in some way, and in that I learn from him. - **Ralph Waldo Emerson**

BJORN BORG QUOTES:

I used to be very bad. I used to throw racquets, swear and do all sorts of stupid things. Eventually my parents told me that, unless I calmed down, I'd never get anywhere in the game. The situation reached a stage where, if I missed a point, I'd get mad at myself and then hit the next three points into the fence on purpose. I was crazy.

I lost a lot of matches because of my temper. Then I learned to behave and felt much better. Now I'm very patient. I don't throw racquets anymore. The turning point came when I started to realize the tennis life isn't so bad. I was thirteen at the time and I told myself: I'm going to have to live with this for the next fifteen years so I had better learn to live with it. Since then I've had no problem. In fact, I'm a very emotional man, even on the court, but now I always keep my feelings locked up inside me.

When you go on the court you hate everyone. It is the way it has to be. I pushed myself. It came from my heart. I wanted it for myself. I wanted to win. Even in practice.

I feel that I have a little bit of an advantage when I play Guillermo because I have been beating him so many times and so easily. I was not scared, because I know he doesn't have that much confidence coming in. He prefers to play from the back, as I do . . . We do everything about the same, but I think I do it a little bit better.

When I was 26 it came to a point I did not enjoy playing tennis anymore. I didn't have the motivation, I wanted to try other things in life, experience other things in life. I was well recognized all over the world. Sometimes you want more privacy with the family. Maybe that was one of the reasons I retired. I still love tennis, follow tennis.

John (McEnroe) and I respected each other. Tennis was very fortunate to have two different personalities with different play styles and we could play great tennis. I think the people enjoyed that very much. We are very good friends, very special thing. Even though we had a great rivalry, we are great friends.

The greatest moment of my career? Winning the fifth Wimbledon. against John, that particular match, it meant a lot for me, for tennis, for John.

I will try so hard to win. I will do everything to win. I have lost here (WCT Dallas, Texas) twice, and I want so badly to win. I have not felt like this before, not like this time. I think Guillermo wants badly to win. But I know how badly I want to win.

We were both fighting for the number one in the world in tennis, but we respected each other. John respected me and I was probably the only guy who respected him out of all the people in tennis history. So we have got a good feeling from each other, but after the tennis we really became very good and close friends, with the families, we call and see each other. That's very rare in sports in general. We understand each other, we know tennis, we played tennis, we had a great career.

Sometimes there should be two winners. That's tennis.

Borg Stats

Career ATP Record: 654-140 in singles, 93-89 in doubles.

ATP Titles   66 in singles, 4 in doubles.

Height: 5-11

Weight: 160

Davis Cup Record: 37-3 in singles, 8-8 in doubles.

Singles Record at the Majors: Australian 1-1, Roland Garros 49-2, Wimbledon 51-4, US Open 40-10.

Career prize money: $3,655,751

Sweden Mystery: Where Have All The Tennis Vikings Gone?

By Scoop Malinowski November 10, 2021

Back in the 1980's and 1990's Swedish tennis was flourishing with an array of champion calibre talents. There was Stefan Edberg, Thomas Enqvist, Magnus Larsson, Magnus Gustafsson, Thomas Johansson, Niklas Kulti, Jan Gunnarson, Anders Jarryd, Thomas Hogstedt, Niclas Kroon, Peter Lundgren, Kent Carlsson, Henrik Sundstrom, Jonas Svensson, Jonas Bjorkman, Mikael Tillstrom, Mats Wilander and Magnus Norman. These numerous Swedish champions followed the trails blazed by Bjorg Borg's eleven Grand Slam titles.

But the Viking spirit and soul of Sweden has been transformed into a different, less awe-inspiring example.

Today there are only two Swedish players who are making a minor impact in the ATP World Tour - 23 year old Mikael and 25 year old Elias Ymer, who lost yesterday as a wildcard in the first round of Stockholm to Frances Tiafoe in straight sets. Leo Borg also received a wildcard but was defeated by Tommy Paul 62 64.

167 ranked Elias Ymer has won 22 ATP main tour matches and was once ranked 105 in 2018.

His younger brother Mikael, not playing Stockholm this week (he's playing an ATP Challenger in Roanne, France) is currently ranked 93. The brothers did win a Stockholm doubles titles together a few years ago, the last time any Swede has won any ATP title, to the best of my knowledge. Mikael has won 39 ATP matches and his best ranking was 67 in March of last year.

Leo Borg, the son of Bjorn, is just 18 years old but having a difficult time progressing to the ATP circuit from ITF juniors. Right now he's ranked outside the top 2000. At French Open and US Open junior tournaments this year, Borg lost in third round in Paris and first round in New York.
How and why Sweden is no longer able to produce world class professional tennis talent is not easily explained. There are still excellent professional

hockey players - Elias Pettersson, Gabriel Landeskog, Elias Lindholm - who star in the NHL - and golfers Henrik Stensson, Alex Noren and Jonas Blixt who win pro golf tournaments.

Unfortunately I can't give any explanation for this dilemma. Critics can blame the Federation, coaching or the mindset of the young athletes of Sweden but nobody knows for sure what the problem is or who deserves blame, otherwise this mass failure could be corrected.

For those who can remember the golden, glory days of Swedish tennis, it's a perplexing mystery why Swedish players are struggling to excel or even make it to journeyman status.

All great things must come to and end and it appears Sweden's days of being a Tennis Super Power have come to that point of evolution.

Nicolai Herlofson: The most important - and violent - Vikings came from Norway and Denmark. The Swedes were never true berserkers. Casper Ruud qualifed in Turin and Holger Rune in Milan. But true, not much has happened after Robin Søderling who disapperead too early. But he remains the only player to beat Rafa at Chatrier by hitting right through him on slow clay court. Rafa's other two losses there haven't happened in that manner.

Scott Smith: I think countries go through periods of success and then drought... Look at the biggest tennis nation... Where are all the top American male players since Agassi, Sampras and Courier?

Peter Bengtsson: It is a big question that every Swede involved in tennis has been asked for many years now. Nobody is sure, no big serious investigation has been made so people tend to make their own take on this. I have my opinions...

Johan Billgert: I have thought about this for many years. I don't have the answer. What might have happened is that we became comfortable and just expected new players to appear in world top - without any real backup and support. To become a top player you can't do it by yourself anymore, like you probably could between 1920-1960's. Just my view and don't actually know of course...

About The Author

Mark Scoop Malinowski was born in Philadelphia, PA and tried playing tennis at Packanack Lake in Wayne, NJ as a teenager but a double bagel loss at the club tournament with friend Kevin Dolan to two girls named Stacy Bradshaw and Karen Rudeen proved to be the end of the tennis dream. Until over a decade later he tried again and eventually reached a top five ranking in the USTA Eastern Section Open Division in 2016 and a no. 1 ranking in the 35s in 2018.

Facing Bjorn Borg is Scoop's eleventh tennis book...

Facing Federer
Facing Nadal
Facing McEnroe
Facing Andy Murray
Facing Hewitt
Facing Sampras
Facing Marat Safin
Facing Serena Williams/Steffi Graf (Double book)
Close Encounters With Donald Trump
The Book Of Joy
Facing Guillermo Vilas
Marcelo Rios: The Man We Barely Knew
Muhammad Ali: Portrait of a Champion
Heavyweight Armageddon: The Tyson vs Lewis Heavyweight Championship Battle
Facing Bob Probert
80's Hockey Biofiles

You can read Scoop's tennis coverage at www.tennis-prose.com and his Biofile interviews at www.mrbiofile.com

DEDICATION

This book is dedicated to my dear father Eugene Robert Malinowski who passed away suddenly on November 24, 2021.

Special thanks to everyone who took the time to share their memories and experiences with Bjorn Borg, the ATP World Tour, and photos from Fila, Diadora, Juan Coronel, Tim Taylor, Leif Shiras, Rob Koenig, Don Berry. Artwork by Alberto Ramirez Suarez, LeRoy Neiman, Andres Bella.

Whatever you can do or believe you can do, begin it, for boldness has genius, power and magic in it. - **Goethe**